Low Blood Sugar Making You a Nutritional Cripple?

by Ruth Adams
and
Frank Murray

Larchmont Books
New York

NOTICE: This book is meant as an informational guide for the prevention of disease. For conditions of ill-health, we recommend that you see a physician, psychiatrist or other professional licensed to treat disease. These days, many medical practitioners are discovering that a strong nutritional program supports and fortifies whatever therapy they may use, as well as effectively preventing a recurrence of the illness.

Contents

Introduction

LET ME START by getting one thing straight. The commonest condition I am called upon to treat in my private practice of internal medicine is low blood sugar (hypoglycemia).

I know this to be true because I perform glucose tolerance tests on every new patient and the results of this testing actually do show that the *majority* of my patients do not have normal curves, but, instead, have findings consistent with the diagnosis of low blood sugar. But, more to the point, I know this because I place these patients on my own version of an anti-hypoglycemic diet with megavitamin therapy, and the majority of them improve dramatically in regard to the various presenting complaints for which they sought help.

Just in case it is argued that patients who see me represent a pre-selected sampling because of my known interest in hypoglycemia and obesity, I can't help recalling that my own office and writing staff, who came to me as workers, not patients, has been similarly tested, and eight out of twelve of them demonstrated low blood sugar and a good response to a low carbohydrate diet.

And I am not alone. At a recent Las Vegas medical convention, the prevalence of this condition was under discussion and every physician who reported doing glucose tolerance testing routinely, also commented on the extreme frequency with which he found hypoglycemia. There were dissenters to be sure, but in every case they were doctors who did not routinely perform the test.

I have every reason to believe, therefore, that low blood sugar is with us in epidemic proportions.

But yet, the American Medical Association, along with

the American Diabetes Association and the Endocrine Society saw fit to publish, in four different medical journals, a strongly worded position statement indicating that hypoglycemia is an extremely rare condition. Since this quadruple publication is an unparalleled event in medical annals, it is a rare doctor, indeed, who did not read their statement to the effect "that there is no good evidence" that "hypoglycemia is widespread" or that it "causes depession, chronic fatigue, allergies, nervous breakdowns, alcoholism, juvenile delinquency, childhood behavior problems, drug addiction or inadequate sexual performance."

You are about to learn through the journalistic efforts of Ruth Adams and Frank Murray, a team with a distinguished record of bringing up-to-date facts about nutrition medicine to the public, *just how much evidence* there really is that hypoglycemia is widespread and that it *does* cause fatigue, depression and many other conditions which can affect your life and health.

Why, then, are these medical organizations so militantly opposed to your doctor recognizing that you have hypoglycemia if you have it or to his even considering the possibility that you may have it?

Particularly when the treatment usually involves nothing more than your following a proper diet?

We can only speculate as to their reasons, but, since one of them is not that they are interested in *your* welfare, it is probable that their reasons involve self-interest.

For one thing, organized medicine has long been supported by their economically powerful ally—the drug industry. At present, about half of the AMA's outside revenue comes from the advertising support of the pharmaceutical industry. And the leaders of this industry know that they can maintain their multi-million-dollar profit picture only if the medical profession continues to consider drugs as the first line of defense in patient care.

It is not hard to imagine how these leaders might react to the prospect of drug therapy being replaced by another modality of health protection of widespread applicability, less expensive and infinitely greater safety. They would oppose it with all their influence, much as the tobacco industry tried to dissuade us from all evidences that cigarette smoking is harmful. Well, such a health modality is upon us, making inroads and dramatic breakthroughs in all of the healing arts. It is the science of clinical nutrition, or nutrition medicine, which is based on the principle that illness can be treated and, in particular, prevented, by improving upon an improper diet.

There can be no question that the widespread acceptance of nutrition medicine as the first line of defense against illness would be seen as a major threat to the drug industry. And in this particular struggle the medical-pharmaceutical combine has an even more powerful ally— the food industry. For the basic precept of nutrition medicine is that the diet we consume has become inadequate, thus creating the very need for the use of nutritional correction. And so the food industry becomes culpable for many of the disease epidemics that ravage our society.

Thus the food industry joins the war against nutrition medicine, rather than submit to changing their practices, well-established on principles of greatest profitability. And their weapons are stronger, for they have under their financial aegis, the important nutrition leaders, and newspaper columnists, as well as the leading nutrition journals themselves. But more significantly, as the leading sponsor of advertising, they have the power to determine which viewpoints may be presented to us through the media—TV, magazines, newspapers. Thus, it is essentially only through books such as this one that we may learn of the vast strides taken by nutrition medicine.

But what of hypoglycemia? Why does the food industry, drug industry, organized medicine axis want us to believe it is so rare? Simply this. Low blood sugar is the denominator common to most of the conditions amenable to nutrition therapy in competition with drug therapy. It is caused by faulty diet and corrected by an improved diet; thus its very existence is an indictment of the present-day American diet.

If our leaders admit to the true prevalence of low blood sugar, they must then admit that drugs should be our *second* line of defense, and they must admit that our food products and consumption patterns must be changed. Specifically, those powerful industrial combines purveying sugar, flour and soft drinks must admit that their very existence, like that of the tobacco industry, carries with it a major health hazard.

Consequently, it would not be surprising if your own doctor, who has been subtly influenced through his medical education, the repeated denial of low blood sugar's existence in his journal reading, as well as the same media we have all been exposed to, whitewashing our national diet, may be reluctant to investigate the diagnosis of hypoglycemia or even to recommend the good nutritional practices which correct it. Further, now that malpractice suits have become his most distressing problem, he may even be fearful to take a position opposed by his leadership.

If so, you may have already sought his help for complaints mentioned in this book as possible conditions caused or aggravated by low blood sugar, and received no solution to your problem. In such a case, this book might prove to be more useful to you than your own doctor has been. Never could I state that self-ministrations from a book, any book, should take priority to visiting a physician who can question you, examine you and take laboratory tests on you specifically.

But, sometimes, leads we get from books direct us to accurate diagnosis and proper therapy. A knowledgeable patient can make his doctor a wise man.

Although I ofttimes approach the dietary management of low blood sugar somewhat differently from the recommendations this book offers, I, nonetheless, have a vast amount of respect for the many scientific studies and medical reports brought together to form the thesis of this book.

Reading it, one begins to grasp the many areas of health and medicine touched upon by low blood sugar and its nutritional correction.

Adams and Murray's book certainly provides food for thought. Or, more accurately, it provides some guidelines to learn which *foods* might just provide you the best ability to *think*.

ROBERT C. ATKINS, M.D., P.C.

May, 1975

New York, New York

CHAPTER 1

Are You a Victim of Low Blood Sugar?

"THE SUGAR-LADEN American diet has led to a national epidemic of hypoglycemia, an ailment characterized by irrational behavior, emotional instability, distorted judgment, and nasty personality defects. Almost 10 per cent of the population is hypoglycemic," state Dr. E. Cheraskin, Dr. W.M. Ringsdorf, Jr. and Arline Brecher in their excellent book, *Psychodietetics: Food as the Key to Emotional Health*; published in 1974.

Still another expert, Dr. Robert C. Atkins, in his 1972 best-seller, *Dr. Atkins' Diet Revolution*, says that "Addictive people seem to have one thing in common: an underlying hypoglycemia. We certainly see hypoglycemia in sugar addicts, in alcoholics, in coffee addicts. People who have studied hard-drug addicts report to me that hypoglycemia is common among them. Cola beverages have long been addictive for many people." He added that "A sugarholic should be told that he cannot afford to have anything—even salad dressings and soups—containing sugar. This can trigger off a binge. Most overweight people wouldn't be thus affected, but a significant number will."

"Hypoglycemia has been estimated to affect 10 per cent of the United States population," states Dr. Harvey M. Ross in *The Journal of Orthomolecular Psychiatry* (Vol. 3, No. 4. "Any other disease affecting even a lesser amount of people would be classified *easily* as an epidemic. But, because this disease is not understood by the general medical population, it is dismissed as a 'fad' disease, and patients who beseech their physicians for a five-hour glucose-tolerance test are oftentimes scoffed at. It is important to know that hypoglycemia is a real disease that can be treated effectively, and relatively inexpensively. It is a disease that will not kill you, but may make you wish you were dead," Dr. Ross says.

What is this insidious disorder known as "hypoglycemia?" It's roughly the opposite of diabetes and is also known as low blood sugar. Prolonged low blood sugar can lead to convulsions and death. And, in addition to a possible cause of alcoholism and drug addiction, hypoglycemia has been related to epilepsy, asthma, multiple sclerosis, rheumatic fever, peptic ulcer, nervousness, fatigue, some forms of mental illness (schizophrenia, for example), heart disease, allergies and many other disabilities.

In diabetes, it is thought that the body does not produce enough insulin—a secretion of the pancreas, which helps the body to use sugar and other carbohydrates—so that levels of sugar become so high that sugar may overflow into the urine.

Low blood sugar is exactly the opposite. The body glands manufacture too much insulin, so that blood sugar levels are entirely too low most of the time. Since many important functions of the body (chiefly those involving the nerves and the brain) depend upon sugar in the blood, they may actually become sugar-starved in such a condition. Obviously, such a state may have serious consequences, as we have noted.

According to *Psychodietetics*, symptoms of hypoglycemia include "dizziness, fainting or blackouts, headaches, fatigue or exhaustion, drowsiness, narcolepsy (abnormal attacks of sleepiness), muscle pains and cramps, cold hands and feet, numbness, insomnia, breakdown, inability to concentrate, excessive worry and anxiety, depression, forgetfulness, illogical fears, suicidal thoughts, tremors, cold sweats, inner trembling, uncoordination, convulsion, fast and/or noticeable heart beat, blurred vision, allergies, itching and crawling sensations, neurodermatitis, arthritic pains, gastrointestinal upsets, loss of appetite, loss of sexual drive and impotency."

Continues *Psychodietetics*: "Spells of low blood sugar give rise to other widely assorted difficulties: dry or burning mouth, ringing in the ears, shortness of breath, peculiar breath or perspiration odor, poor memory, temper tantrums, noise and light sensitivity, nausea and hot flashes. A typical hypoglycemia victim is, in fact, an emotional yo-yo, strung out on a chemical reaction he cannot control, with reactions so severe they frequently resemble insanity."

The diabetic may be given a manufactured insulin to make up for the secretion which he cannot produce himself. If he gives himself too large a dose, he may suffer from insulin shock: perspiration, great nervousness and anxiety, trembling, fatigue and, finally, possible death.

If the low blood sugar patient goes too long on an inadequate diet or too long without eating, he may induce much the same kind of condition in himself. Or the symptoms may take on a number of the violent and bizarre forms that we have just enumerated. In any case, these diseases may be the aftermath of several years of low blood sugar levels.

If these disasters are caused by too little sugar in the blood, the best diet to overcome them would seem to be a diet rich in sugar. In the early days of experimentation, doctors used to give their patients sugar when they found that hypoglycemia was present. They gave them candy or glucose tablets to eat whenever they felt the symptoms of low blood sugar returning.

For a time this seemed to work, until, gradually, the patients found that they needed the sugar supplements almost all the time. They kept them on bedside tables and ate them whenever they awoke during the night; they carried them about all day and ate them constantly. If they did not, the unpleasant and dangerous symptoms returned shortly after meals.

Those are the two key words to hypoglycemia: "after meals." Symptoms are always improved by eating—no matter what. But when the meal is loaded with sugar and starch, symptoms return after several hours or perhaps less. So the doctors took another look and decided to try a different kind of diet.

Perhaps the same diet prescribed for diabetics would work for hypoglycemics? Sure enough, a diet high in protein, with sugars and starches omitted or cut to a minimum, and with a moderate amount of fat, steadied the wild swings in blood sugar readings so that the badly affected patient could eventually go from breakfast to lunch without any symptoms, from lunch to dinner without any complications. He was essentially cured. And the diet was approximately the same diet a diabetic would have to follow.

The spacing of meals is important to a hypoglycemic, as it is to the diabetic. He must eat frequently. In the diet prescribed by Dr. Seale Harris—and later made famous in the book *Body, Mind and Sugar*—the low blood sugar patient must take four ounces of fruit juice or an orange or grapefruit immediately upon arising, eat a high-protein breakfast, take four ounces of juice two hours after breakfast, a high-protein lunch, then eight ounces of milk three hours after lunch and four ounces of juice an hour before dinner. After a high-protein dinner, he must take eight ounces of milk within 2-3 hours, then four ounces of milk or a small handful of nuts every two hours until bedtime.

By high-protein diet we mean the following: meat, eggs, fish, milk, cheese and other high-protein foods in normal quantities, plus all vegetables except potatoes, and all fruits except those mentioned below. They may be cooked or raw, with or without cream—but without sugar.

Only one slice of bread or toast may be eaten at any

meal; spaghetti, rice, macaroni and noodles are forbidden. Salad greens of all kinds, mushrooms and nuts may be eaten as freely as desired.

For beverages, any unsweetened fruit or vegetable juice (except grape or prune juice), weak tea, decaffeinated coffee, coffee substitutes, club soda, distilled liquors are allowed.

Absolutely forbidden on the diet are: candy and other sweets such as cake, pie, pastries, sweet custards, puddings and ice cream; caffeine—either as strong tea, coffee or soft drinks containing caffeine; potatoes, rice, grapes, raisins, plums, figs, dates, bananas, spaghetti, noodles, macaroni and other pasta foods, wines, cordials, cocktails and beer—and, of course, sugar.

An added word is perhaps necessary about the caffeine. Dr. E.M. Abrahamson, the physician co-author of *Body, Mind and Sugar*, tells in his book of patients whose blood sugar-regulating mechanism was so sensitive to caffeine that even one cup of coffee would undo the benefits of weeks of painstaking dieting. If you are such a person, you would do well to substitute decaffeinated coffee or some other beverage for coffee because, apparently, there is no hope of your ever being able to drink coffee or strong tea without inviting a low blood sugar crisis.

Dr. Abrahamson does not mention this, but other researchers have discovered that cigarettes do the same— lower your blood sugar. This may be one reason why you "need" a cigarette soon after you have put the last one out. If your dependence on nicotine is such that you grow faint, tired, nervous when you don't smoke, chances are that low blood sugar may be to blame. Obviously, it's time for you to give up smoking.

It is easy to see that the daily routine followed by millions of people is creating nutritional cripples insofar as blood sugar levels are concerned. The individual who eats no breakfast, or takes only coffee or coffee and something sweet—like a doughnut or Danish—then lights up a cigarette, has started the vicious cycle.

Within an hour or so, his energy is ebbing, his nerves are on edge, he's tired, restless. It's coffee-break time. The combination of caffeine, a sweet bun and another cigarette shoots his blood sugar levels up to a new high. He feels fine for a short time. But soon the levels are plunging down again and the symptoms return. If he skips lunch or eats a lunch consisting mostly of carbohydrate, he will have another period of fatigue, jitters, nervousness, restlessness or possibly headache in the late afternoon. If he takes another coffee break, with some easily assimilated carbohydrate, the symptoms will recur again before dinnertime.

At dinner he gets the sugar-regulating mechanism back to normal for a time with some protein food, but, if he has been eating this way for years, the blood sugar levels will swing wildly down again by bedtime. They will reach their lowest point during the night or early morning.

By breakfast time our patient is grouchy, headachy, tired. He may even be trembling and faint. The breakfast coffee and cigarette bring the blood sugar up and restore him—but not for long. As the situation becomes worse, the periods of comfort grow shorter and shorter. After the first time he has blacked out at the wheel of his car, the sufferer will have to see his doctor.

So many physicians refuse to recognize the existence of a diet-induced condition such as low blood sugar that a foundation—Adrenal Metabolic Research Society of the Hypoglycemia Foundation, Inc., P.O. Box 98, Fleetwood, Mount Vernon, New York 10552—has been organized to publicize this condition and help to combat it. The group is headed by dedicated individuals who got into health trouble themselves because of a diet that led to low blood sugar. Working alone and without the financial backing most national health organizations have, they are doing an excellent job in spreading the word about hypoglycemia. If you feel so inclined, why not send them a contribution.

Incidentally, you have noticed that the list of forbidden foods on the low blood sugar diet includes such excellent foods as figs, dates, raisins, plums, bananas, etc. This does not mean that these are harmful foods—only that they should not be taken while one is trying to re-educate all the complicated mechanisms of glands and digestion involved in the low blood sugar condition. After you have the mechanism regulated, you can, of course, begin to take these foods again—in moderation.

Now that you understand a little more about the complexities of hypoglycemia, let us proceed with some specific instances where low blood sugar is a contributing factor to many debilitating diseases. And if 10% of the American population does have hypoglycemia, it might explain why so many of us have heart attacks, cancer, allergies, peptic ulcer, fatigue, multiple sclerosis, etc. It might also explain the reason why so many of us become alcoholics, schizophrenics, drug addicts, suicides—and why crime is on the increase.

CHAPTER 2

Sugar and the Health of Your Heart

AS LONG AGO as 1933 a researcher, Dr. J. H. P. Paton, wrote in the *Lancet*, the respected British medical journal, theorizing that the great increase in the intake of refined sugar in recent years may be the cause of the great increase in coronary heart disease and heart attacks. Dr. Paton concluded that "there is a group of diseased conditions—obesity, arteriosclerosis (hardening of the arteries) and diabetes—which have long been associated clinically, and which are increasing in modern times, although the general death rate is falling. Is it not possible that this increase is directly associated with excessive carbohydrate intake which is largely, if not entirely, due to the prodigious increase in the use of sugar?"

In the 42 years since that time, we have witnessed the rise of the theory that dietary cholesterol is the most important dietary factor in heart and circulatory diseases. The word "cholesterol" strikes terror to the hearts of people who fear heart attacks. Doctors put their patients on diets in which fat from animal sources is cut down to almost nothing because that is where the cholesterol occurs. Along with meat, cream and whole milk, eggs are outlawed or almost outlawed on such a diet. Meat, whole milk and eggs are among the most valuable foods, nutritionally speaking. They contain not only large amounts of high grade protein, but also B vitamins and minerals in abundance. Eggs and whole milk also contain vitamin A.

Evidence accumulates that we may be nearing the end of this era in "dieting." New evidence seems to show that dietary fat as such cannot be the only cause or even the chief cause of heart and artery conditions. Dr. Fred A. Kummerow reported at a meeting of the Institute of Food Technologists in May, 1974 that he has fed the new artificial, cholesterol-free egg mixtures to animals with disastrous results. All of the offspring of his laboratory rats which were fed with the new product died within a few weeks of weaning. The experiment seems to show that something mighty important is missing in the cholesterol-free eggs.

Another speaker at the same meeting, Dr. David Kritchevsky of the Wistar Institute, told of studies on the effect on cholesterol of fiber in diets. He pointed out that fibrous diets decrease the threat of cholesterol by sweeping the cholesterol out of the digestive tract before it has a chance to enter the bloodstream. Modern white bread contains little fiber, said he, whereas wholegrain bread has a lot. So do fruits and vegetables, especially green, leafy vegetables, beans, wholegrains and potatoes.

Other studies reported at the same meeting showed that cholesterol in meals had almost no relationship to blood cholesterol. One scientist reported that animals on low cholesterol diets developed gallstones. Said the *Philadelphia Inquirer*, reporting on the meeting, "The researchers generally agreed that the simplistic advice to 'cut down on eggs, fat, etc.' no longer makes good nutritional sense in view of recent research. There's far more to the mystery of cholesterol and heart disease than what we eat, they said."

The Journal of Nutrition, June, 1974, reports that a 65 per cent sugar diet fed to rats during their initial post-weaning period has long-lasting effects on their fat metabolism, even though this high-sugar diet was not fed during the last half of the animals' lives. The study indicates that the kind of carbohydrate fed during early days may have important effects on the way one's body handles fats during all the rest of one's life.

In a lengthy article in *The American Journal of Clinical Nutrition*, April, 1974, Dr. Richard A. Ahrens of the Food, Nutrition and Institution Administration Department, College of Human Ecology at the University of Maryland, relates the history of the controversy over diet and coronary heart disease. He says that cigarette smoking, obesity, sedentary life and stress have all been implicated as possible causes of our rising figures on heart attacks. But "the most striking dietary change (in the past 100 years or so) has been a sevenfold increase in the consumption of sucrose (sugar)," he says.

In charts and tables, Dr. Ahrens shows clearly the relationship between high sugar consumption and circulatory diseases, including high blood pressure. "A number of animal studies have found that replacing starch calories with sucrose effectively shortens the average lifespan," he says. Additional disease changes that have been attributed to high sugar intake are increased stickiness of blood cells that might predispose to coronary thrombosis (heart attack), also an unhealthy increase in size of the liver, and gallstones, as well as tooth decay and nephrosis, which is perhaps related to the effects of sugar on the kidneys.

Dr. Ahrens talks about the role of the trace mineral chromium in heart and circulatory conditions. He points out that the trace mineral chromium is removed entirely when sugarcane is refined into white sugar. The effects of this removal of chromium from diets in which there is much white sugar seem to involve severe disturbances in the way the body uses carbohydrates. The chromium appears to be essential for the body's successful handling of sugar. When there is a deficiency of chromium, giving this trace mineral appears to be very beneficial, says Dr. Ahrens. We wonder how anyone who eats the amount of sugar most Americans eat (more than two pounds weekly) could possibly not be deficient in chromium.

A great deal of work has been done collecting information on the heart attack rate among people who eat varying amounts of sugar. For 10 years or so, different scientific workers have reported different conclusions. In some cases, heart attacks have been directly related to high sugar consumption. In the case of the Yemenites who migrated to Israel, heart attacks were almost unknown among them. Their diets in Yemen contained almost no sugar. After they arrived in Israel their sugar consumption rose steadily and so did the number of heart attacks.

Says Dr. Ahrens, in conclusion, "It is relevant to observe that the pandemic of arteriosclerotic heart disease continues to increase on a worldwide scale in rough proportion to the increase in sucrose consumption, but not in proportion with saturated fat consumption."

The final link in the chain of evidence is a new book by a British physician who has been saying for many years that sugar and refined white flour and cereals are the main cause of most of our degenerative health troubles, Dr. T.L. Cleave, Surgeon Captain of the Royal Navy. Dr. Cleave's book is *The Saccharine Disease*. The title does not refer to the artificial sweetener, but to sugar and refined starches.

Dr. Cleave says that people who have heart attacks, diabetes, obesity, tooth decay, varicose veins, hemorrhoids, peptic ulcer, gout, hiatus hernia, simple high blood pressure and colonic disorders of many kinds are all suffering from "The saccharine disease." All those disorders could be prevented, he claims, by simply eliminating from our diets foods which have been concentrated by removing their fiber-sugarcane and cereals chiefly.

With arguments that are sensible and reasonable, Dr. Cleave presents his case. When foods are over-refined, he says, we eat too much of them. Our bodies have no way of knowing how much to eat, since they are descended for millions of years from many ancestors whose food contained large amounts of fiber. Four or five apples contain the same number of calories and the same amount of sugar as several chocolates. You can easily eat a lot of chocolates since they have no fiber. You feel stuffed when you eat a large amount of apples. The fiber they contain prevents you from eating too much.

Dr. Cleave buttresses his arguments with well-researched material on primitive people who have almost no troubles with diseases like those listed above until they move to "civilized" areas and begin to eat "white man's food." The incidence of gallstones, heart attacks, diabetes, obesity and so on rises almost at once and within 20-25 years is as high as it is among white people—or higher.

For many years a steadfast physician in North Carolina has been telling the world that heart attacks are caused by low blood sugar. The Fall, 1974 issue of *Homeostasis*, the publication of the Adrenal Metabolic Research Society of the Hypoglycemia Foundation, published the good news that this physician, Dr. Benjamin Sandler, recently read a paper before the International College of Angiology, stating that the fundamental cause of anginal syndrome and myocardial infarction is a sharp fall in the blood sugar to hypoglycemic levels in non-diabetics and to relative hypoglycemic levels in diabetics.

Translated into laymen's language, this means simply that two of the most dangerous heart conditions (angina and myocardial infarction) are caused by low blood sugar levels. In the non-diabetic these attacks occur when blood sugar levels plunge way down. And in diabetics they occur when blood sugar levels fall relatively low.

Angina is the terrible, sharp chest pain sometimes radiating down the shoulder and left arm which occurs usually after physical effort or emotion. Doctors give nitroglycerin to relieve it. It happens because the heart is getting too little oxygen and blood. Myocardial infarction is a lack of blood in some part of the heart muscle, causing damage to that part of the heart. Either of these conditions can be, and frequently are, fatal. Less serious attacks require careful treatment and lengthy recuperation.

SUGAR AND YOUR HEART

The editor of *Homeostasis* hails Dr. Sandler's address as "the most important report of our time." We are inclined to agree. Heart attacks kill more people than any other condition in our country and in all Western industrialized countries. In all these countries, sugar is consumed in astonishing amounts by almost everyone. Individual "average" Americans eat an estimated 120 pounds of sugar a year. Since many people do not eat sugar—babies, diabetics, those on reducing diets, those who have no craving for it, etc.—this means that many people who do eat sugar eat far more than 120 pounds annually. Some nutrition experts have reported analyzing individual diets which include 400 pounds of sugar yearly.

The Establishment has for years been blaming our fat consumption for heart and circulatory disorders. Millions of people have cut their fat to dangerous levels, fearful of the very sound of the words "cholesterol" and "saturated fat." But the incidence of heart attacks has not decreased. Government bureaus, heart societies, the American Medical Association and other professional groups continue to preach that we must stop eating eggs, milk and meat (all fine, nourishing foods) and change over to unsaturated fats, commercial cereals and other foods which contain almost no fat. But it is extremely difficult to plan such diets to include enough protein. Dieters tend to eat cottage cheese at every meal and not much else. They grow weary of the monotony and make up for it usually by stuffing on starchy and sugary foods. Almost no one is warning them, officially, of the dangers of these foods.

For over 30 years Dr. Sandler has been writing and speaking on the subject of low blood sugar in relation to heart attacks. He published a landmark book, *How to Prevent Heart Attacks* (unfortunately now out of print), which outlines his theories on exactly how low blood sugar produces the conditions that lead to heart fatalities. In the book he tells us of a medical paper which appeared in 1954, written by the famous heart specialist, Dr. Paul Dudley White, and Dr. Fredrick Stare of Harvard University. In the paper these savants marveled at the suddenness of our epidemic of heart attacks. This condition was almost never seen before the beginning of this century.

The authors said, "To realize that the first cause of death in the United States is a disease little known 50 years ago comes as something of a surprise to physicians and public alike... No disease has ever come so quickly from obscurity to the place coronary heart disease now occupies, to maintain itself there with a permanence presumably to endure in this country for years to come."

The secret of this sudden attack, according to Dr. Sandler, is the suddenness with which sugar became available very inexpensively. Our individual consumption of sugar rose from 44 pounds a year to well over 100 pounds annually within 50 to 75 years. Today, we are eating vast amounts of the white stuff and the heart attack figures continue to climb.

The editor of *Homeostasis* asks, "If hypoglycemic attacks can cause heart attacks and the hypoglycemic diet can prevent heart attacks, one of the greatest life-saving breakthroughs will be accomplished. However, there is a big IF in this whole situation. The IF is will the associations devoted to heart take up the challenge?"

It seems obvious that the answer is No. Part of the reason, we must suspect, is that many of the researchers and physicians who head these nationwide groups are getting money from the giant food industry which makes most of its profits selling those very foods which are forbidden on the diet to correct low blood sugar. Government bureaus of professional men and women are supported with financial grants from this industry. The sugar industry, the soft drink industry, the vast agricultural conglomerates which control most of our food from the moment the seed is sown until the final product appears on the supermarket shelves, have terrific political clout. Their lobbyists (such as the aforementioned Dr. Fredrick Stare), their donations to political campaigns, their friendly help to legislators on favorite projects—all these things go a long way toward influencing legislation. Their gifts to national associations control the position these groups take officially on matters of diet in relation to heart conditions.

What foods would not move from supermarket shelves if everyone in the country were to go on a diet to prevent hypoglycemia? Practically everything in the way of packaged and processed foods must be forbidden on such a diet. The only foods the hypoglycemic can eat are fresh foods—meat, fish, poultry, eggs, dairy products, plus fresh vegetables, fruits, nuts and seeds. White sugar and refined carbohydrates are out. Commercial cereals, loaded with sugar in one form or another, are forbidden.

The diet which Dr. Sandler recommends to prevent heart attacks is very simple, easy and inexpensive to follow. It requires no special recipes. You eliminate from your meals all foods that contain the quickly absorbed carbohydrates (sugar and refined starches mostly) and you eat considerable amounts of protein and moderate amounts of fat. *You must eat often during the day so that you do not become hungry and fatigued.* Snacks must be high-protein snacks.

Here is the diet to correct low blood sugar. This is from Dr. Sandler's book, *How to Prevent Heart Attacks.* All animal food may be eaten in unlimited quantity. This means beef, pork, lamb, mutton, veal, poultry, fish. They may be eaten fresh, dried, canned, smoked. Eggs may be used freely. All dairy foods may be eaten in unlimited quantity—cheese, buttermilk, yogurt, butter and so on.

These foods should be eaten in reduced quantity because they contain considerable carbohydrate: dried beans—the kind you use for baked beans—lima beans, macaroni and all other pasta like spaghetti, rolls, bread, biscuits and crackers, corn, split peas, potatoes, sweet or white, lentils, rice, noodles and all cereals.

These fresh fruits should be eaten in limited quantity— that means no more than one piece of fruit at a meal because of their sugar content: citrus fruits, peaches, melons, apples, pears, pineapple, strawberries, all berries, grapes, cherries, plums. Fruit juices, canned and dried fruits, and preserved fruits should be avoided. Tomato juice is allowed.

These foods may be eaten in any quantity since they contain little starch: artichokes, asparagus, avocados, bamboo shoots, string beans and wax beans, red beets, broccoli, brussels sprouts, cabbage, carrots, cauliflower, celery, swiss chard, cucumbers, eggplant, endive leaves, beet greens, dandelion greens, turnip greens, kale, kohlrabi, leeks, lettuce, mushrooms, okra, onions, parsley, parsnips, fresh peas, peppers, pumpkins, radishes, rhubarb (unsweetened), spinach, summer squash, tomatoes, turnips, watercress, pickles, horseradish, mustard, vinegar, olives, capers, mayonnaise. Nuts may be eaten in unlimited quantity, except for chestnuts, peanuts and cashews, which contain considerable starch.

These foods must be eliminated *entirely* from your diet: sugar and all foods that contain it, soft drinks, ice cream, sherbets, canned and preserved fruits, cakes, cookies, candies, pastries, pies, fruit juices, jams, jellies, marmalades, custards, syrups and any and all other foods that contain sugar. You must read labels of any packaged, canned or frozen foods and buy nothing that has sugar in it.

Breakfast must be high in protein: fresh fruit or tomato juice, eggs, any kind of meat or cheese or fish in any quantity. Only one slice of bread if desired. Lunch must be high in protein. Tomato juice or broth, plus meat, fish, poultry, or cheese or milk, in any quantity, plus any permitted vegetables, raw or cooked, salad with or without dressing, no more than one slice of bread. Dinner is essentially the same as lunch. One piece of fresh fruit may be eaten with any meal.

Dr. Sandler allows coffee and tea if no sugar is used. More recent research suggests that coffee be eliminated, except for decaffeinated coffee. Scientists have discovered that the caffeine in coffee and strong tea disorders the blood sugar levels. Cigarettes do the same, so the low blood sugar victim or the individual who wants to avoid a heart attack must avoid smoking. Why not put the heart attack candidates in your family on this diet and see how much better they feel?

A letter in *Homeostasis* stated: "My husband was placed in the hospital with the finding of... heart block. He was found to have hypoglycemia. The doctor has no recommendations. However, my husband changed his diet to the hypoglycemic diet. Life was completely changed for the better. My husband was a different man. However, because the doctor didn't stress the diet, my husband decided the diet had nothing to do with his recovery. He dropped the diet. Now he is back where he was to begin with."

CHAPTER 3

Alcoholism and Low Blood Sugar

"EXPERIENCE SHOWS THAT when an alcoholic succeeds in getting off alcohol he usually substitutes sweets," writes Dr. Robert C. Atkins in *Dr. Atkins' Diet Revolution*. "This is because almost all alcoholics are hypoglycemic, and sugar provides the same temporary lift that alcohol once did."

Dr. E. Cheraskin and Dr. W. M. Ringsdorf, Jr. add in *Psychodietetics*: "A great many researchers who have lifted the alcoholic off the couch and placed him under the microscope are convinced that uncontrolled drinking is a metabolic disorder that can be treated by nutritional therapy."

They continue: "Doctors are, of course, aware of the fact that alcoholics frequently suffer from malnutrition. But as Dr. Roger Williams points out, they assume the malnutrition to be the result of the alcoholism, not a contributing factor. Malnutrition of the brain cells is simply not considered as a *cause* of alcoholism."

Writing in the *Journal of the American Geriatrics Society* for February, 1966, Dr. John W. Tintera, then living in Yonkers, N.Y., believes that the crux of the alcoholic problem can be traced to low blood sugar. The condition exists, he says, whether it occurs in the social drinker who already has a problem with carbohydrates (which alcohol aggravates); the predisposed person who inherits his weakness; the chronic alcoholic; or the recovered alcoholic who has physical and personality debilities. For a non-alcoholic, a night of heavy drinking is apt to produce low blood sugar the following morning. But for the alcoholic, this condition can be chronic.

It is a rather common notion that alcoholics craved candy and other sweets when they were young. They often went on sweet-eating binges, because they found that it temporarily cured their depression or fatigue. This craving for sweets, Dr. Tintera points out, and which Dr. Atkins corroborates, is obviously a manifestation of low blood sugar. When the alcoholic found that alcohol could produce the same effect as sugar, he became a heavy drinker.

Of course, the problem drinker soon discovers that the cessation of his troubles was, unfortunately, only temporary, thus it becomes necessary for him to drink most of the time in order to feel comfortable and happy. And the children of alcoholics tend to become alcoholics, too, Dr. Tintera says. Or else the children become total abstainers, since they realize that they cannot cope with carbohydrates successfully.

Low blood sugar involves an increased output of—or, perhaps, an increased sensitivity to—the insulin that is produced in the body. This sensitivity can be intensified by stress, exhaustion, pressure, fatigue, violent exercise or emotional turmoil. In his article, Dr. Tintera explores the many ramifications of low blood sugar and how it can affect other glands. He discusses the "dry jitters," which are alarming nervous crises that afflict reformed alcoholics who have been unable to correct their low blood sugar condition. As a result, their livers and adrenal glands do not function normally. He notes that it is rather common to find members of Alcoholics Anonymous carrying a lump of sugar or a candy bar with them in case they have an attack of the dry jitters.

If these reformed alcoholics are left to work out their own problem, they quite naturally adopt a diet that is high in carbohydrates, believing that this will alleviate the jitters, Dr. Tintera goes on. "But in no instance have we found these patients to be free of low blood sugar."

In another part of the article, Dr. Tintera discusses the relation between alcoholism and drug addiction, a growing problem in the United States and around the world. He tells the story of a young man whose father was a chronic alcoholic and whose mother suffered from low blood sugar. In order to support his heroin addiction, the boy became a thief. While in prison the boy was given a blood sugar test, which showed that he was suffering from hypoglycemia. Doctors gave the boy a high-protein, low-carbohydrate diet and glandular treatment, which corrected the low blood sugar. He was no longer a drug addict, but the officials had a problem. Should he be released, should he be sent to prison, or should he remain at the state hospital? Dr. Tintera says that, because of their condition, alcoholics tend to become addicted to barbiturates.

In an earlier book, *Megavitamin Therapy*, we explore the relationship between low blood sugar and alcoholism, drug addiction, schizophrenia and hyperactivity in children in greater detail. In essence, the documentation in that book is along the same lines as suggested by Dr. Tintera. But, in addition to a high-protein, low-carbohydrate diet, the specialists quoted are also using mega-doses of certain vitamins with startling results. Dr. David Hawkins of the North Nassau Mental Health Center in Manhasset, N.Y., and Dr. Abram Hoffer of Saskatoon, Saskatchewan, Canada, are two specialists in this field with extremely good credentials. Although drug addiction has tapered off a bit in recent years, a growing number of young people, especially pre-teen and teen-agers, are turning to alcohol, because it is cheaper and easier to get. Invariably, these youngsters are also "sugarholics."

Getting back to Dr. Tintera, he continually stresses that,

in dealing with hypoglycemia, what is important is not the point *from* which the blood sugar level falls or the point *to* which it falls, but rather the *suddenness of the fall*. This is the cause of the symptoms which make all of the trouble. And, as Dr. Sandler suggests, it often triggers a heart attack. The high-protein, moderate-fat diet—in which the easily assimilable carbohydrates are forbidden—tends to alleviate this rapid plunge from one level to another. Both protein and fat are assimilated slowly, so there is ample time for the process of assimilation and absorption to proceed normally, and for all the organs and glands to function normally. Consequently, no part of the blood sugar regulating mechanism is suddenly confronted with a considerable load of pure carbohydrate (sugar or alcohol), which overburdened it and caused the disasters which are apt to follow if blood sugar levels take a sudden plunge.

Alcoholics are generally heavy smokers, and, through nervous habit, smoke about two packs of cigarettes a day, Dr. Tintera says. "As the patient begins to feel better, he can easily limit smoking to specific periods, such as after dinner, and really enjoy it," he adds.

In spite of the fine work that is being done by Alcoholics Anonymous and other groups, some alcoholics suffer a relapse. Following a period of abstinence, the alcoholic appears physiologically normal, and yet he has a relapse. This condition always amazes psychologists and psychiatrists, Dr. Tintera says. However, he is amazed that anyone who has not corrected the basic physiological difficulty can remain sober. If the person is a member of AA, he has to awaken each morning resolving not to drink for 24 hours, and his entire orientation must be geared to this demand.

Of course, if the reformed alcoholic can be convinced of the effectiveness of the low blood sugar treatment, he can get up each morning "with a purpose and joy in being alive—not with a feeling that it is another day of struggle. He now has a reserve to withstand emotional stresses and has the satisfaction of being able to master any situation he is likely to encounter," Dr. Tintera says.

"The aim of the treatment," Dr. Tintera continues, "is restoration of homeostasis (balance) for all the endocrine (gland) factors involved. Therapy consists chiefly of the administration of adrenal cortex extract, adequate nutrition and psychologic guidance. Diet is of extreme importance. Initially a rather high fat content is allowed, but eventually the diet should be high in protein, moderate in fat, and low in readily available carbohydrates."

This simply means a diet from which carbohydrates

Here is Dr. Tintera's diet list. It is similar to Dr. Sandler's but is worth repeating:

Foods Allowed

All meats, fowl, fish and shellfish.
Dairy products (eggs, milk, butter and cheese).
All vegetables and fruits not mentioned below.
Salted nuts (excellent between meals)
Peanut butter, oat and jerusalem artichoke bread.
Unflavored gelatin with whipped cream.
Sanka, weak tea and sugar-free soft drinks.
Soybeans and soybean products.
Oatmeal.
Certain high-protein macaroni and spaghetti.

Foods to Avoid

Potatoes, corn, macaroni, spaghetti, rice, cereals.
Pie, cake, pastries, sugar, candies.
Dates, raisins and other dried fruits.
Cola and other soft drinks.
Coffee and strong tea.
Alcohol in all forms.

(sugar, flour, etc.) are eliminated, as well as those vegetables, nuts, fruits and legumes which are high in carbohydrates. We can eat as much as we want of almost everything else. For the alcoholic, of course, he must abstain from all alcoholic beverages, coffee and strong tea.

Dr. Tintera selected the foods that are allowed because of their high protein content. Peanuts and soybeans are high in carbohydrate, but he apparently feels that their protein content will insure the patient that the carbohydrate is released so gradually during the digestion process that little damage can be done to the blood sugar regulating mechanism. And the kinds of food that Dr. Tintera recommends have their own built-in guarantee against over eating.

Thus, we see a close relationship between obesity and alcoholism. To deter the jitters caused by low blood sugar, one person may take to soft drink or candy binges, while another will turn to alcohol. If the first kind of person does not correct his blood sugar condition, he is likely to become fat. The other kind of person is destined to become an alcoholic.

CHAPTER 4

Cancer and Blood Sugar Levels

"THE AFFLUENT AMERICAN DIET, already indicted as a major factor in heart disease, now is being linked to another mortal ailment—cancer of the colon and rectum," states Jerry E. Bishop in the October 25, 1973 issue of *The Wall Street Journal* .

"Studies have reached the point where there is little doubt that the diet is somehow related to the risk of getting colon-rectal cancer," Bishop says. "In recent weeks one study has put the spotlight on beef. Other research is implicating fat. One theory pinpoints refined flour and a lack of roughage."

Bishop added that, at the time of his article, 99,350 Americans were expected to get this type of cancer in 1974, up from 86,000 new cases five years before. Deaths in 1974 were anticipated at 48,000, up from 44,000 five years previously, he says.

When cancer experts talk about the various kinds of cancer in human beings, they emphasize the absolute necessity for discovering a test that will indicate a tendency to get cancer—a susceptible state, you might say. Once we know how likely a person is to get the disease, we can possibly bring to bear all the preventive measures known and prevent the cancerous condition from doing any damage. Many researchers are working in laboratories trying to perfect such a test.

Meanwhile, a very practical, down-to-earth physician at the University of Alabama Medical Center is working directly with patients to see if he can find some way of predicting which group of people is most susceptible to the disease. Dr. E. Cheraskin, whom we have already mentioned, and his colleagues published an article, "Cancer Proneness Profile," in the August, 1969 issue of *Geriatrics* .

One fairly uncomplicated test which can be performed in a laboratory or a clinic is the glucose tolerance test, which, as we know, reveals how the blood sugar level of the patient may vary in comparison with the average or normal condition.

In two earlier experiments, Dr. Cheraskin's group found that those subjects whose blood sugar was higher (hyperglycemia) tended to report more cancer incidents. Those whose blood sugar levels were consistently lower, with advancing age, had fewer cancer illnesses to report. The newer experiment involved 507 patients who had taken part in a Diabetes Detection Drive. As their blood sugar levels were being monitored, these people were given a form to fill out, indicating whether a doctor had ever treated them for a tumor or a cancer.

The answers were then studied statistically and some interesting facts emerged. First, it was obvious that, with advancing age, cancer incidence increases. People below 29 years of age reported no cancer. Second, those people from 30 to 50 years of age who suffered from low blood sugar reported the most cancer. Third, in the oldest age category—from 50 on—the incidence of cancer went up at exactly the same rate as the incidence of high blood sugar, indicating diabetes or a tendency to diabetes. Fourth, in all categories, overweight appeared to be closely related to cancer incidence.

The Alabama researchers believe their evidence shows that the people with low blood sugar when they are middle-aged tend to get diabetes after 50. That is, the blood sugar disruption which produces one kind of disorder in middle-age produces an opposite manifestation of it as you grow older. This is not surprising, for the body attempts at all times to maintain all its functions at normal level. Perhaps its efforts to keep blood sugar levels normal up to the age of 50 are disrupted even further by all the various stresses that occur later on, so that the whole mechanism finally fails and diabetes results. In any case, the diabetes figures are closely related to the cancer figures in the older age groups.

What these scientists appear to have turned up is evidence that perhaps the same patterns of life which produce the low blood sugar and later high blood sugar also produce the cancer, or at any rate produce such a condition in the body that the person becomes an easier cancer victim. A further confirmation of these facts is that the incidence of all these disorders is going up at a frightening rate, even as our national load of overweight and obesity increases steadily year after year.

Dr. Cheraskin does not suggest in his article what one might do to prevent the disorders of blood sugar levels which appear to be so closely related to cancer-proneness. He is suggesting only a test that could be used to spot this susceptibility and possibly forestall future tragedies. But in his later book, *Psychodietetics*, Dr. Cheraskin and his co-authors say: "No one would deny that malignant growths within the body are evidence of the breakdown of its resistance to disease-causing factors. But even in the case of a disease as serious as cancer, providing the body with a superabundant supply of all essential nutrients will not only help ward off external attacks but also increase chances for recovery."

Dr. Cheraskin adds that this was proved conclusively in 1966, "by dramatically improving the rate of response in a group of cancer patients subjected to a radiation therapy with just one week of the psychodietetic approach—the Optimal Diet and nutrient supplementation."

The experimental group consisted of 54 female patients

with biopsy-proven cervical cancer. They were all scheduled for radiation therapy at the Tumor Clinic in the University of Alabama Medical Center. But one week before the radiation treatments were to begin, one-half of the women were placed on a diet that was high in protein, low in refined carbohydrates, plus a vitamin-mineral supplement potent enough to insure an excess of essential nutrients. The other 27 women, given neither supplements nor a diet regimen, served as the control group.

About three weeks after the end of the radiation therapy, "the control group showed an average radiation response of 63.3, normal for such treatment according to previous hospital records, with patient response ranging in degree from 0 to 100. Forty per cent of the group displayed unfavorable scores; thus their prognosis was very poor.

"In contrast," Dr. Cheraskin and his co-authors report, "the experimental group averaged a 97.5 response. Scores ranged from a low of 91 to a high of 100; every patient showed a favorable response to the therapy, thus a good chance for survival.

"If one week of 'supernutrition' can affect cancer recovery in such a spectacular fashion," the authors say cheerfully, "your best defense against any kind of stress—environmental, psychological, physical—is obvious: keep your nutritional status as high as you possibly can."

Getting back to low blood sugar, we already know what prevents it. It's just a matter of diet and times of eating. If we can prevent the low blood sugar before the age of 50, doesn't it seem probable that we would also prevent the high diabetes incidence after the age of 50, since both are manifestations of the same problem? And if we can prevent both of these, don't we have a very good chance of stopping that upward curve of cancer incidence which, at present, indicates that one person out of every four in America will have cancer at some time in his life?

We have already given you a diet to regulate blood sugar levels. To further control blood sugar levels, experts insist on snacks between meals. But these must be high protein snacks, nothing sugary or starchy. And a high protein snack in the evening will keep blood sugar levels up during the night so that there will be no morning headaches or grouchiness when you awake the next morning. You, of course, know to avoid coffee, strong tea, soft drinks, cigarettes.

Dr. Cheraskin's research that was reported in *Geriatrics* was partially financed by a branch of the American Cancer Society. Don't you wish they would publicize the findings widely, thus possibly preventing many future cancer tragedies?

CHAPTER 5

Mental Health and Diet Are Related

"IT IS BECOMING increasingly apparent that diet is an important tool in the treatment of mental illness," states a letter to the editor in the December 19, 1973 issue of *Medical Tribune*. "A diet very low in carbohydrate and free of sugar increases the efficacy of the tranquilizers and antidepressants. In megavitamin therapy, where very high doses of vitamins are used (B3, C, B6) remissions are obtained more rapidly when the patient follows a diet with less than 60 grams of carbohydrate a day. As improvement is noted, small amounts of carbohydrate are added. Elimination of sugar from the diet is essential."

Judge Tom R. Blaine, a state district judge in nine Oklahoma counties, wrote a book called *Goodbye, Allergies* (which we discuss in another chapter), in which he described the way he cured his own lifelong allergies with a diet and injections of adrenal extracts. In the process of following the diet (which is the same high protein diet used to treat low blood sugar), Judge Blaine became absorbed in the subject of low blood sugar and its possible relation to other disorders in addition to allergies.

In his professional life he had dealt with many disturbed human beings, many criminals, alcoholics, schizophrenics, drug addicts. Is it possible, he asked, that the reason for some of these terrible personal tragedies may be simply an unsuspected low blood sugar condition? He began to do research on the subject, corresponded with many professional leaders in fields of psychiatry and medicine who were already using the diet in the treatment of many assorted emotional, physical and mental illnesses.

The result of his research was another book, *Mental Health Through Nutrition* , dealing with "Hypoglycemia, the Ignored Disease," "Vitamins Bring Mental Health," "Schizophrenia Responds Favorably to Vitamin Therapy" and many related subjects. The evidence he has collected is a formidable indictment of modern diets, loaded as they are with refined foods and white sugar. Judge Blaine has turned up facts from many corners of the earth. All are well documented. He gives names and titles of the people he quotes. Because he is a judge, rather than a professional scientist or physician, his writing is easy for the layman to follow. There are no complex biological terms or concepts. There is extensive information about the diet for treating low blood sugar and how to follow it.

Judge Blaine has turned up some information not generally available in most books on the subject. He says, for example, "Dr. Joseph Wilder of New York, specialist in psychiatry and neurology, found that low blood sugar is far more serious with children than it is with adults. Dr. Wilder said, 'The importance of nutrition for mental functioning is much greater in children than in adults.'

"In adults, faulty or insufficient nutrition may alter or impair specific or general mental functions, and eventually cause reparable or even irreparable structural damage of the central nervous system. In children, we face a grave additional factor. The development of the brain may be retarded, stopped, altered, and thus the mental functions may become impaired in indirect and not less serious ways. . . .

"The child may be neurotic, psychopathic, and be subject to anxiety, running away tendencies, aggressiveness, a blind urge to activity and destructiveness, with impairment of moral sensibilities...In its simplest form, it is a tendency to deny everything, contradict everything, refuse everything, at any price." Does this sound like anything you read in your local newspaper or see on TV?

The book does not deal only with youth. Judge Blaine is aware of the fact that, as we grow older, there is a tendency toward eating less nutritious diets and we are apt to reward ourselves with more empty calorie sweets. The aging brain and nervous system need protein, vitamins and minerals in perhaps even larger amounts than younger persons need. He tells us stories of near miracles worked in old folks with good, nourishing diet and plenty of vitamins and minerals.

The sections on schizophrenia are enlightening. Judge Blaine includes letters from patients and their families describing their condition before and after treatment with megadoses of vitamins and the diet to correct low blood sugar. These are patients of Dr. Abram Hoffer, Dr. Humphrey Osmond and other pioneers in the use of this kind of treatment for schizophrenia.

The book is well provided with names and addresses of helpful organizations in this field, names and addresses of physicians who use this treatment, books to read, professional books to get your doctor to read, and several valuable appendices with information on vitamins, minerals and so on. It's a fine beginner's book on the subject of the dietary treatment of low blood sugar and the use of megadoses of vitamins for treating many emotional and mental disorders.

In researching our book, we came across this letter from a Ph.D. who teaches at a leading Eastern university. The ACE injections which she mentions are injections of adrenal hormones which stimulate the adrenal glands. For more information about this method of treatment of low blood sugar, write to the Adrenal Metabolic Research Society of the Hypoglycemia Foundation, P.O. Box 98, Fleetwood, Mount Vernon, N.Y. 10552.

"When I arrived at my new job some nine years ago, I

41

had just recovered from an almost fatal hemorrhage," she writes. "I was extremely weak. Several people who met me then thought I had not long to live. I was on a bland diet. My staples were plain crackers and buttermilk. The doctor had instructed me to squeeze all the juice from any ground meat I ate and permitted me to have a variety of soft cooked vegetables.

"I soon began to have difficulties with vision and several times was on the verge of fainting. A friend put me in touch with a doctor who made extensive tests, including the 6-hour glucose tolerance test. Finally, the hypoglycemia which some of my friends had already diagnosed became an established fact. The new doctor gave me injections of ACE (adrenal-cortico-extract) and B complex of vitamins. I had fortunately been on a diet which had enough protein and leafy green vegetables. With the help of the ACE I began to regain energy and my digestive troubles began to disappear. Difficulties with vision were almost gone.

"One of the vision troubles was a recurring pattern of jagged light lines and a very stylized whorl of small checks. This latter hallucination seems to be a typical symptom of schizophrenia. I also had frequent feelings of slight shock, of unreality and dissociation which sometimes accompany schizophrenia. It is difficult to describe the emotional vulnerability, the instability and total discouragement of the earlier times. I knew I could not rely on my own judgment and vision and was terrified to drive a car. I was also unreasonably irritable and often wild with frustration because everything I did seemed so difficult. I still cannot explain even to myself how I managed to keep hard at work and do what I felt was an almost adequate job.

"In addition to the injections and diet, I was most fortunate in the psychological support with which I was blessed. My friends' acceptance of me even when some of my reactions must have been incomprehensible was more than any human being deserves.

"Recently I realized that I am now practically 'normal' and, considering that I am 63, I am doing far better than could have been expected. In several tests of my physical and mental stability, I have come through with flying colors.

"I recently talked with a psychiatrist friend and several people who have or have had hypoglycemia or who have hypoglycemic relatives. The consensus is unanimous that the three most important factors in treatment are psychological support, diet and ACE therapy. We who have had the disease know our abnormal sensitivity to insult or rejection. Shortly before my own illness, I had a series of traumatic rejections or 'failures'. My friends and family sustained me throughout with utmost patience and understanding. It's true that a healthy sense of humor helps.

"One of my friends has a hypoglycemic wife who escaped with him from Hungary and broke down in the process of escape and resettlement. The kindliness and intelligent support this man shows his wife is, I believe, what keeps her out of a mental institution. He never reprqaches her, although she does unreasonable things, suffers intense depression and can be irrationally irritable. She won't stick to her diet. My psychiatrist friend believes that the schizophrenia which is associated with hypoglycemia is, in many cases, a retreat or withdrawal from the intolerable pain that is caused by unappreciative friends or relatives who lack the insights and 'tender loving care' necessary for the afflicted person to cope with the emotional syndrome resulting from the endocrine (gland) and metabolic imbalances.

"My own physician explained the reluctance of many doctors to give the glucose tolerance test. It puts a great strain on the patient, who may go into coma. There are often frequent changes in blood sugar level and metabolism, which makes the test results uncertain. Hypoglycemia is a symptom of several organic disorders and its causes may be very complex. The effects of the ACE injections cannot be controlled and may have unpredictable side effects and after effects, because so little is known

43

about the functions of the pancreas and blood sugar regulation.

"I am utterly delighted that I am at last able to do the job I have done, that I still have a very good store of energy, that I can eat a great variety of interesting food and that my spirits are excellent."

According to a UPI dispatch on March 25, 1971, a former college coed filed a $1½ million lawsuit against the State of California and a number of other defendants claiming that she was wrongly confined in a state mental hospital as a schizophrenic for five years.

In 1965, the young woman enrolled in a state college after graduating with honors from her high school. She reported to the college health center, complaining of migraine headaches. She was diagnosed as having schizophrenia and was committed to the state hospital, where she was treated with drugs and electro-shock treatment.

Her weight dropped to 80 pounds and she grew much worse. Finally, she was transferred to a medical center where her illness was diagnosed as low blood sugar. As we have noted, it is the sudden fall in blood sugar which is apparently responsible for the migraine headaches, the dizziness, the fatigue, etc. And such a condition can mask schizophrenia and a long list of confining illnesses. Surely such a horror story as the one told by this young woman cannot be justified in the light of the simplicity of the treatment, and the fact that low blood sugar has been known as a widespread disorder for many years.

In his book, *Nutrition Against Disease*, Dr. Roger J. Williams says that "Vitamin B12 is definitely a link in the nutritional chain that protects against mental disease. In pernicious anemia, caused by deficiencies of this vitamin, the mental symptoms are by no means uniform; they can range from such mild symptoms as having difficulty in concentrating or remembering to stuporous depression, severe agitation, hallucinations, or even manic or paranoid behavior.

"Like the symptoms in pellagra," Dr. Williams continues, "those caused by B12 deficiency may be very similar to those observed in schizophrenia. Yet the relationship between pernicious anemia and B12 is not simple; other factors may be involved as well. Sometimes administering B12 will clear up the mental symptoms associated with pernicious anemia rather slowly—and occasionally, incompletely. The relationship between vitamin and disease is not as direct as in the case of pellagra."

Regardless of what the specialists may use to treat schizophrenia—niacin, vitamin B12, vitamin B6, vitamin C, zinc, manganese, lithium (chiefly for depression), etc.— they must first correct the patient's diet. And that diet is often the same one to correct hypoglycemia.

The official position of the psychiatric establishment is that diet and vitamins have nothing to do with mental health. Yet in *Clinical Psychiatry News* for August, 1974, we read, in two separate articles, that abnormal blood sugar levels were responsible for behavior problems in children and psychotic adults. Forty-four out of 48 children suffering from hyperactivity, learning disability and depression had symptoms of low blood sugar. And low blood sugar was found in twice as many psychotic patients as in patients who were merely neurotic. The cure for low blood sugar, of course, is not to eat more sugar, as many children and adults do; the treatment is to dispense with sugar and all foods that contain it, to omit beverages containing caffeine, to stop smoking and to follow the high-protein diet.

CHAPTER 6

Toothache May Be
Related to
Low Blood Sugar

DID YOU EVER wonder why, in ancient paintings and portraits, you seldom see the subject smiling? The Mona Lisa's smile is world-famous, but it is only a half-hearted smile. Her mouth is firmly closed. Pictures of Queen Elizabeth I, England's celebrated Queen who gave her name to the golden period of English history, had her portrait painted many times. But in every likeness, her mouth is closed.

The probable reason for these closed-mouth portraits is discussed in a fascinating article in the *Journal of the American Dental Association*, May, 1967, entitled "Elizabethan Toothache: a Case History." The author states that, throughout the 45 years of her reign, the great queen suffered from decayed and diseased teeth which tormented her night and day, and may have been responsible for her death. Literature of the time, letters and journals speak frankly of the queen's dental problems.

Beginning with a troublesome time while her permanent teeth erupted, Elizabeth went on to suffer from rampant tooth decay, chronic toothache, facial pains and gum deterioration. Often these conditions became so noticeable that state visitors could not help but comment. Many times audiences and state occasions had to be cancelled because the queen was suffering from intense toothache.

On one occasion when her pain had endured for many days and nights, depriving her of sleep, the doctors recommended pulling the decayed tooth. But Elizabeth could not face the pain of the operation. Anesthetics of any kind were unknown at the time. Teeth were pulled usually by barbers, men who accompanied jugglers and clowns to fairs where they pulled teeth, clad in fantastic costumes with a belt of teeth swinging around their waists.

Because of the queen's abhorrence of pain, a good friend, the Bishop of London, who was an old man, offered to have one of his teeth pulled to show her that the pain was quite endurable. Contemporary descriptions of the queen, commenting on her beauty, fine posture and gracious ways, could not avoid adding that her teeth were "yellow" or "black;" many of them were missing. In her portraits, the deterioration of her mouth structure becomes sunken, the fine, oval face shortens and, eventually, the queen appears jowly and heavy.

No methods of repair or replacing teeth were known, of course, except to treat aching ones with (probably) ineffective herbs and potions. So the richest and most glamorous queen in Western history had to live her life in pain, not only actual physical pain from her rotting teeth, but also psychological pain, for she was vain and could not help but know how the blackened, rotting teeth spoiled her looks.

There seems to be no doubt as to the cause of Queen Elizabeth's condition. It is mentioned in many of the ancient quotes in the JADA article: "her teeth are black (a defect the English seem subject to, from their too great use of sugar)." An Elizabethan historian of modern times tells us that Elizabeth was inordinately fond of sweets and carried some kind of confection with her wherever she went. In many portraits she is carrying a small bag, something like a muff, and it is thought she may have carried her confections in it.

The poor condition of the teeth of most rich people in the Elizabethan period came through to us because of the many recipes in herbals of that time for breath-sweeteners, mouthwashes and tooth-whiteners. Teeth were cleaned (when they were cleaned at all) by rubbing them with a cloth. Toothpicks were sometimes used. Gold toothpicks were popular among the nobility and were often used as jewelry.

Elizabeth's death is believed to have been caused by a "septic condition arising from the mouth." This could certainly be an infected tooth or teeth which, with no antibiotics or knowledge of hygiene and infections as we know it today, would most likely have been a common cause of death.

The poor classes in Elizabethan England seem to have suffered hardly at all from the dental and gum troubles of the nobility. They could not afford sweetmeats or sugar. Their food consisted mostly of black bread made from completely whole-grain flour. They had some meat and vegetables with lots of chewy foods like lentils and dried beans. The consistency of their food must have been helpful in preventing tooth and gum troubles. It was rough and coarse—the kind of food that is most effective in preventing decay and gum disorders. Vegetables were looked down on by the gentry because they were simple, unsophisticated food not fit for refined, snobbish tastes.

It must be remembered, too, that scurvy, which was apparently very prevalent, especially in winter, must have played a considerable part in the gum and tooth troubles of the Elizabethans. No one knew the value of fresh fruits and vegetables to prevent scurvy. And scurvy (the disease of vitamin C deficiency) has dire effects on teeth and gums. Teeth loosen; gums become flabby, swollen and bleeding.

In *The Englishman's Food*, J.C. Drummond and Anne Wilbraham, commenting on the destruction of teeth due to the use of sugar by the Elizabethan nobility, say: "It rather looks as if this was a popular view, even at this date, and that it had arisen from the observation that the rich suffered more than the poor and an obvious difference between their diets was the relatively large amount of sweetmeats which the former could afford." And they quote a contemporary historian, Paul Hentzner, who wrote, in 1598 of sugar: "The immoderate use thereof, and also of sweet confections and sugarplummes, heateth the blood . . . rotteth the teeth, maketh them look black."

Because of her insatiable sweet tooth, did Queen Elizabeth have hypoglycemia in addition to her decayed teeth and unusual sensitivity to pain? We will probably never know. But doctors and dentists do know that different people have different sensitivity levels where pain is concerned. Pain which one person may not even notice may prostrate someone else in paroxysms of anguish. Some people are able to endure near-fatal wounds without flinching. Others faint at the sight of a dentist's drill or hypodermic needle, because they anticipate such terrible pain.

Dr. W.M. Ringsdorf, Jr. and Dr. E. Cheraskin, of the University of Alabama, read in medical literature of the special pain diabetics suffer from sensitive teeth, especially when the teeth are struck. They wondered if the same condition might prevail with people suffering from normal levels of blood sugar or levels that are chronically low.

In experiments which they conducted, Drs. Ringsdorf and Cheraskin came to the conclusion that both diabetes and low blood sugar cause more than average pain in dental patients. They tested nine patients whose teeth are abnormally sensitive and nine with teeth seldom bothered by pain. They gave each group a 3-hour glucose tolerance test. If one is diabetic the reaction to a heavy dose of sugar (glucose) is followed by sky-rocketing blood sugar levels which remain high. If one has low blood sugar, the usual reaction is that the blood sugar shoots up rapidly and then falls rapidly to dangerous levels.

The Alabama researchers found that abnormal pain was associated with both very high blood sugar levels and very low blood sugar levels, They pointed out that such characteristics will not become apparent in the average test of this kind, since the very low figures of the hypoglycemic people will pull down the very high levels of the diabetics, so that the "average" will appear to be somewhat near normal.

This may be one reason, they think, that other researchers have difficulty pinpointing other disease symptoms as being associated with either very high or very low blood sugar levels. On an individual basis, however, some of the figures are very revealing. One graph shows a blood sugar level that sky-rocketed from 39 to 84 milligrams per 100 milliliters within one half hour of taking the sugar, then plummeted to 9 milligrams three hours later. Such a low level of blood sugar would be capable, it seems to us, of producing many unpleasant and dangerous symptoms.

Abnormal sensitivity to pain may be one of these symptoms. It may be that the individual who gets through what would be excruciatingly painful experiences without batting an eyelash may have an ideally well-regulated blood sugar mechanism, while the person who flinches with pain very often has a disordered mechanism for handling blood sugar levels. They may be either too high most of the time, or too low. In either case, friends and family may decide the pain is psychological or psychosomatic and may tell the doubled-up sufferer to pull himself together and behave like an adult.

In a letter to the editor of *The Journal of the American Medical Association*, January 6, 1974, the Alabama physicians remind their physician readers that, "If prevention of chronic disease is to become a reality, the scientific community must recognize the importance of maintaining the physiocochemical characteristics of the body's internal environment within narrow limits." In other words, doctors must begin to realize that when efficiently-run body mechanisms are purring along as they are meant to, chances are the patient will be healthy. When any mechanism is so disturbed that the results of tests show either too high or too low a level of this or that important body substance—then that patient is sick.

The single most important word to be used in connection with good health, then, is *homeostasis*, the maintenance of "steady states" by the proper coordination of all physiological processes. All organ systems are integrated by automatic adjustments to keep within narrow limits those possible disturbances caused by internal changes, or something that comes from outside the body. And the result of such a change, in the susceptible person, may be either excessively high or excessively low blood sugar levels, resulting in unexplained pain in the teeth, as one of the accompanying symptoms, or in one or more of the disorders that we discuss in this book.

CHAPTER 7

Do You Have a Dry Mouth?

THE MEDICAL WORD for a dry mouth is *xerostomia*. It is a condition in which not enough saliva is produced. It may be the result of taking drugs which stop the flow of saliva, or it may be due to a depressed mental state, with not enough saliva as one of the symptoms.

Dry mouth frequently affects older folks—in their 70s and 80s. Anyone who has this condition should stop taking such a drug or drugs, if he has been taking them. If mental or emotional upset is the cause, the reasons for this should be found and corrected, if possible. Vitamin A is sometimes helpful in increasing the amount of saliva, according to *Health in Later Years*, by Dr. Robert E. Rothenberg.

Another possible cause of dry mouth was discussed in the July 29, 1974 issue of *The Journal of the American Medical Association*. Dr. E. Cheraskin and Dr. W.M. Ringsdorf, Jr. talked about people who have dry mouths and also disorders of blood sugar regulation. It is well known, they tell us, that diabetics frequently suffer from dry mouths.

One researcher, testing a group of diabetics and a group of non-diabetics, found that the diabetics had only about one-fourth as much saliva as the healthy people. However, asked Drs. Cheraskin and Ringsdorf, isn't it possible that dry mouth may be a symptom of any disorder of blood sugar regulation—either hypoglycemia or diabetes? Unfortunately, there seems to be no way to check this, since few doctors give routine tests for this condition.

Drs. Cheraskin and Ringsdorf got together 38 volunteers, 19 of whom complained of dry mouth, 19 of whom did not have such a problem. After the volunteers were given a glucose tolerance test, Drs. Cheraskin and Ringsdorf found "highly significant" differences among these people. Those with dry mouth apparently included both the hypoglycemic and diabetically inclined people. The healthy volunteers had no feelings of discomfort from dry mouth. The distinction was not easy to spot, for those who had blood sugar that was too low pulled down the blood sugar figures for those whose blood sugar was too high, a condition that we mentioned in conjunction with another experiment by these two Alabama doctors. But, on an individual basis, it was found that both extremes—high and low—tended to occur most often in those whose mouths felt dry.

So it's possible, if you suffer from a feeling of dry mouth, that you may have diabetes or hypoglycemia. Those physicians who recognize the dangers of low blood sugar and correct the diets of patients so that blood sugar levels normalize themselves have the reward of seeing these patients lose the unpleasant and dangerous symptoms and regain good health. The tell-tale symptoms, as we have mentioned, may be dizziness, overpowering hunger, faintness, chronic fatigue, aggressive behavior, heart palpitations, etc.

The answer, of course, is the high-protein, low-carbohydrate diet. Eat something as soon as you get up in the morning. Follow with high-protein meals and snacks for the rest of the day. If you awaken in the night—hungry and faint—get a glass of milk or a piece of cheese or some nuts. The protein will help to adjust your blood sugar levels, the calcium will help you to sleep.

Aren't you likely to put on weight? Not a chance, if you banish forever all the sugary goodies that you used to eat. It's the sugar that makes you fat, just as it disrupts blood sugar regulation. On your high-protein diet—which is also the most nourishing diet you can design—you will find your craving for sugar disappearing gradually, because your addiction to sugar is gradually disappearing.

After six weeks of this kind of diet, check on your dry mouth and see if it hasn't improved. Meanwhile, of course, go to your doctor and have your blood and urine checked to see if you have diabetes. If you do, he will probably put you on a diet similar to the one we discuss in this book.

CHAPTER 8

The "Neurasthenia" of Virginia Woolf

VIRGINIA WOOLF WAS a gifted British novelist and critic who committed suicide in 1941 at the age of 59. In *Beginning Again*, the third volume of her husband's autobiography, Leonard Woolf gives some details of their life together, which seem to indicate that Virginia suffered from low blood sugar and serious vitamin and mineral deficiencies. This was due chiefly to her lack of interest in food and her unwillingness to make an effort to be well nourished.

Mr. Woolf, himself a famous writer, tells us that the mental illness that pursued Virginia through her adult life played a large part in both their lives and was the ultimate cause of her death. The doctors—and they went to many—called her illness *neurasthenia*. Beyond naming it, they could do nothing to alleviate it. According to *The American College Dictionary*, this disorder is a "nervous debility or exhaustion, as from overwork or prolonged mental strain, characterized by vague complaints of a physical nature in the absence of objectively present causes or lesions (wounds)."

"If Virginia lived a quiet vegetative life," says Leonard, "eating well, going to bed early and not tiring herself mentally and physically, she remained perfectly well. But if she tired herself in any way, if she was subjected to any severe physical, mental or emotional strain, symptoms at once appeared which in the ordinary person are negligible and transient, but with her were serious danger signals. The first symptoms were a peculiar headache low down at the back of the head, insomnia, and a tendency for the thoughts to race. If she went to bed and lay doing nothing in a darkened room, drinking large quantities of milk and eating well, the symptoms would slowly disappear and in a week or 10 days she would be well again."

If she did not take these precautions, says Woolf, her symptoms raged for several weeks. And four times in her life she "passed the border which divides what we call insanity from sanity." She suffered from manic-depressive illness. In the manic stage she was wildly excited, her mind raced, she talked incessantly. At the height of the attack she had delusions and heard voices. In the depressive stage which followed, she was "in the depths of melancholia and despair; she scarcely spoke; refused to eat, refused to believe that she was ill and insisted that her condition was due to her own guilt; at the height of this stage she tried to commit suicide . . . In 1941 she drowned herself in the river Ouse."

One of the most troublesome symptoms of her breakdowns, reports her husband, was her refusal to eat. At almost every meal someone had to sit beside her for an hour or more, trying to persuade her to eat a few mouthfuls. By not eating she was, of course, making her condition much worse. He thinks her refusal to eat was motivated by "some strange feeling of guilt; she would maintain that she was not ill, that her mental condition was due to her own fault—laziness, inanition, gluttony." Even when she was not ill, he says, it was extremely difficult to induce her to eat enough food to keep her well.

"Left to herself, she ate extraordinarily little and it was with the greatest difficulty that she could be induced to drink a glass of milk regularly every day. It was a perpetual, and only partially successful, struggle; our quarrels and arguments were rare and almost always about eating or resting," Woolf says.

It was significant, he tells us, that whenever she had finished a book—she was the author of over 25 books, beginning in 1915 with *The Voyage Out*—working with intense concentration, she was in a state of mental collapse and in danger of a breakdown. She had just finished her last book on February 26 and killed herself March 21. It is difficult to imagine a better example of how vitamin and mineral deficiency, plus low blood sugar, combined to destroy this talented, successful individual. Born in 1882, Virginia Woolf lived at a time when nothing was known about vitamins (they were not officially discovered until 1911), and very little was known of the science of nutrition. Mental illness was then considered a form of demon-possession or else a Freudian nightmare brought about by psychotic and guilt-ridden associations with one's family and friends.

How easy it would be for doctors today to cure such individuals with injections of massive doses of vitamins, which could produce good appetite again. A high-protein diet with frequent small meals and plenty of high-protein between-meal snacks could probably have controlled this desperate illness and saved all the anguish it brought to Virginia Woolf and the members of her family.

CHAPTER 9

New Hope for Those Who Suffer from Allergies

IN *Psychodietetics*, Dr. E. Cheraskin, Dr. W. M. Ringsdorf, Jr. and Arline Brecher discuss what Dr. Marshall Mandell calls "ecological mental illness." Dr. Mandell describes EMI as a hypersensitivity to natural and synthetic substances in food, water and air, and says that it is a very common ailment that is often misdiagnosed and incorrectly treated. Over 200 of Dr. Mandell's patients have been relieved of long-standing emotional complaints once specific allergens were removed from their diets, *Psychodietetics* states.

"The complex nature of EMI requires exhaustive testing before allergens can be pinpointed. In one case, that of a 40-year-old man with a history of chronic fatigue, mental confusion and nervous tension, previously diagnosed as psychosomatic, 15 food tests were given," *Psychodietetics* continues. "The results showed that after eating wheat the patient became restless, tense and unable to concentrate; that coffee made him lightheaded and gave him a headache; that chicken produced a 'nervous' reaction characterized by dizziness and confusion; that eggs made him yawn and unable to concentrate; that peas brought on a tired, headachy, flushed feeling; that corn made him tense and irritable. No medication or allergy treatments were necessary. He simply avoids eating the major test-incriminated foods and restricts his intake of the minor offenders. He has been well for over a year."

One of Dr. Mandell's most puzzling cases, according to *Psychodietetics*; was an 8-year-old schoolboy who often fell asleep at his desk. In fact, he performed so badly in school that his teachers had written him off as a chronic daydreamer. Dr. Mandell discovered that the boy was eating a lot of chocolate-flavored foods in the school lunchroom—chocolate milk, chocolate ice cream, chocolate cupcakes, chocolate-chip cookies. The boy was also fond of an oat-flour cereal and had at least two bowlsful before going to school. Oats and chocolate turned out to be the boy's two major allergies, and, as Dr. Mandell explains it, allergy victims often crave the foods that are causing the allergic reactions.

Incidentally, Dr. Ben F. Feingold, a California specialist, believes that many hyperactive, autistic children are allergic to the thousands of chemical food additives that are dumped into our food supply. Often adults can cope with many of these additives, in contrast to a small child who may be eating large quantities of these chemicals and whose little body cannot accommodate these unhealthful substances.

According to some authorities, you inherit your tendency to be allergic. If your mother and father or both are allergic, there is a 50 per cent chance you will be, too. There is a 57 per cent chance of allergy in children who have only one allergic parent. About 15 per cent of modern Americans are allergic to some one thing or many things. Another 25 to 30 per cent are less easily sensitized. About 55 to 60 per cent never have allergies.

Says Dr. Richard A. Kern, in *Archives of Environmental Health*; "The allergic person is born that way and so remains until he dies... He may have eczema in infancy, hay fever in adolescence, then asthma in middle years, and finally eczema again in old age—all of these caused by different allergies."

Dr. Kern goes on to describe allergy as a disease of modern times which is steadily becoming more prevalent as more potential allergenic substances are introduced in our environment. Every new chemical, drug, household product or commercial process is bound to cause someone, somewhere to react allergically. Hunting down and eliminating these allergies becomes more difficult with every passing year.

According to Dr. Kern, primitive people seem to have fewer and less severe allergies than "civilized" man. He presents a fascinating theory which may help to explain this. He describes the Norway rat which has been used in laboratories for more than 100 years. Considering the life span of the rat, this corresponds to 5,000 years in human history.

Some time ago a researcher named Richter decided to examine some Norway rats whose ancestors had been living in laboratories and compare them to wild Norway rats. He found that the adrenal and pituitary glands were much smaller in the laboratory rat—the adrenal cortex being only about one-third the size of the corresponding organ in the wild rat.

It is difficult to make a rat allergic to anything. To do so one must remove most of the adrenal gland. So it appears that this gland must have something to do with one's susceptibility to allergies. The adrenals are the glands that give one the extra spurt of energy and endurance in times of danger. The wild Norway rat needs a full-size adrenal gland so that he can get away from his enemies or fight them to the death if cornered. The Norway rats whose ancestors have lived in a quiet laboratory where there are no enemies or stressful situations have, over many generations, lost most of their adrenal glands. They don't need them, for they never encounter situations where they have to fight or run.

Says Dr. Kern, "One is tempted to believe that man, like

the captive Norway rat, has had to fight less and less for his existence and so has less and less need for his 'fight' and 'stress' mechanism, with a consequent reduction in size and function of his adrenals." Primitive man—much freer of allergies—still lives as he has for centuries, surrounded by all the enemies that have always threatened him. He still needs the power his adrenal glands give him in an emergency to fight or flee. Could the size of his adrenal glands be one reason for his comparative freedom from allergies?

Goodbye, Allergies, the book by Judge Tom R. Blaine which we previously mentioned, seems to bear out this theory. For 60 years Judge Blaine had been allergic to chocolate, many kinds of fruit, peanuts, tomatoes, milk, pollens, dust, feathers, animal hair, gas fumes, aspirin—the list is almost endless.

Treatment with adrenal injections and a diet aimed at controlling the levels of sugar in his blood brought about complete freedom from all allergies. Determined to share the news of his recovery with the rest of the world, Judge Blaine, with the help and counsel of several physicians, wrote his book. He had reached such a state that he was preparing to give up his work. Migraine headaches, fatigue, irritability tortured him. Treatment with adrenal injections and the diet to correct low blood sugar brought a complete cure by 1959—after 60 years of almost continuous doctoring. Four physician friends listened to his story and found four professional reasons for not believing it.

But other allergy sufferers clamored to hear his story. "All of those belonging to that great unnamed fraternity of men and women who from time to time have said to each other, between sneezes, wheezes, nose blowings, coughing, spitting, scratching and yawning, 'You ought to go see my doctor. He cured me.'... Not one of them reported even a partial failure of the... treatments, and every letter and telephone call I got from them was a glowing tribute to the efficacy of the treatment."

The treatment—that is, the injection of adrenal extract—is for the purpose of rejuvenating worn-out adrenal glands so that they can once again respond to stressful situations. This gives one a clue to the fact that allergic attacks, in many people, become worse when they are under emotional stress. If the adrenal glands are worn out, they cannot respond as they should to stress. And one doctor said, explaining the situation, "I'm learning about the intricate and subtle chemistry of the adrenal glands; (scientists) discovered that the differences between the non-allergic majority and the allergic minority was the difference between strong, alertly responsive adrenals which can and do marshal the body's defenses in a flash, and weak, sluggish glands which are incapable of doing what they should."

The functions of all the body's glands are closely related, so it is not surprising to find that the pituitary gland also seems to have a great deal to do with one's susceptibility to allergies. The pituitary is sometimes called the Master Gland of the body. And the pituitary is involved in regulating the amount of sugar in the blood. The adrenals, the pancreas, the liver and other organs are also part of this mechanism, so that a disorder in any one can mean trouble in this department. So can the wrong diet!

And the diet that means most trouble for the mechanics of blood sugar regulation (need we say it?) is precisely the diet eaten by most modern "civilized" people—a diet which is impossible for primitive people, since refined foods, unbuffered by proteins, minerals and vitamins are unknown and unavailable to them. So it seems reasonable to assume that such a diet may have lots to do with the susceptibility of "civilized" man to allergies.

In his book, Judge Blaine, of course, suggests a diet to follow to eliminate allergies. It is the proverbial high-protein, low-carbohydrate diet.

The Oklahoma lawmaker has found that many of the emotional problems of those brought before him are the result of the wrong eating habits. In his book he tells us, for example, that many gland specialists believe that alcoholism is a symptom of a functional disturbance of the adrenal glands. Alcoholics respond well to injections of adrenal extract and the diet for low blood sugar.

"Alcohol is the adrenals' number one enemy," he says. "Someone born with strong adrenals will probably be able to drink heavily for a long time before he becomes alcoholic . . . If an individual was born with weak adrenals, or if his adrenals have been damaged by disease, he will not be able to drink very long until alcohol has done him lasting damage."

Judge Blaine notes that most "cures" for alcoholism feature the frequent eating of sugar or candy. This, of course, restores blood sugar balance for a short time, but it brings about an even worse fluctuation in blood sugar levels, so that it cannot be depended upon for a permanent treatment.

Judge Blaine also points out the importance of minerals in regulating glands and blood sugar levels. Calcium is especially important, as researchers in this field have discovered. During the days when he was still allergic, Judge Blaine could not tolerate milk. So he took bone meal tablets as an excellent source of calcium and other minerals. After his allergies departed, he was able to drink milk again and it became an important part of his diet.

CHAPTER 10

Psoriasis and Blood Sugar Regulation

OF ALL THE mysterious disorders affecting the skin of human beings in the technological age, psoriasis seems to be the most mysterious. After many years of study, medical science still seems baffled by this disorder, which is uncomfortable, inconvenient, disfiguring, but not life-threatening and never fatal.

It's a scaly disease, the silvery scales affecting various parts of the body and, in some cases, almost the entire body. There are 11 duly tabulated kinds and degrees of psoriasis: flexural psoriasis, psoriasis of the scalp, guttate psoriasis, erythrodermic psoriasis, pustular psoriasis of palms and soles of feet, generalized pustular psoriasis, psoriatic arthritis, psoriasis of the nails and mixed skin disorders, with psoriasis as one of the complications.

It is estimated that two to three per cent of us—four to eight million Americans—suffer from this disease, though we do not know for sure, since many victims of the disease conceal their condition because it is unsightly. More women than men suffer from psoriasis. Black Americans and West Africans are almost immune. Anything which disturbs the general health may initiate a flare-up of the skin condition. Anything which promotes a feeling of well-being and relaxation (a happy vacation, for example) tends to improve the condition.

Psoriasis mostly attacks people between the ages of 10 and 50. Medical literature tells us solemnly that there is no cure and the disease will probably continue throughout life, although temporary remissions are to be expected.

Doctors give a number of drugs to psoriasis victims to take internally or apply to the affected areas. None of these is successful in every case and the most they can do is to control the disease, never cure it.

In the nutritional area, investigation has shown many helpful procedures. In 1964, *Medical World News* reported that two Russian physicians were getting excellent results with vitamin B12 combined with folic acid (another B vitamin) and vitamin C. The doctors treated 72 patients with injections of the three vitamins twice daily for 20 days. After a treatment-free period of three weeks, they gave the injections again for another 20 days. Good results followed the first course of treatment in 29 patients, after the second in 25 patients and after the third course of treatment in four patients. The remaining 14 patients reported no improvement. Relapses occurred within six months in 52 patients and after six months in eight patients.

There seems to be no reason why these treatments could not have been prolonged, since these water-soluble vitamins are harmless. They could also have been taken by mouth.

A Brooklyn physician, writing to the *Medical World News*, stated that he has been using vitamin B12 injections along with a proteolytic enzyme in resistant cases of psoriasis with "marvelous results." On the other hand, a 1964 article in the *British Medical Journal* reported no success with vitamin B12 injections. This is the way nutritional treatment often turns out when it is given for short periods and when not enough of the vitamin is given. We do not know how much vitamin B12, folic acid and vitamin C were given or for how long. Today we know that these vitamins are harmless and can be taken in very large doses, with no risk. Perhaps that is essential in stubborn cases.

A form of vitamin A applied to the skin controlled psoriasis, according to an article in *The Journal of the American Medical Association* for March 10, 1969. The University of Miami physicians used it on 26 patients with psoriasis, with excellent results. The doctors say they have read of psoriasis victims using vitamin A orally in doses which were toxic and not getting results. But when "vitamin A alcohol" was applied to the affected area in their tests, improvement was striking.

The *New York State Journal of Medicine* for November 1, 1973 reported the use of retinoic acid on psoriasis. This is a form of vitamin A for applying externally. It has also been used successfully for treating *acne vulgaris*. In 22 cases of psoriasis there was "significant improvement" after the skin treatment. Another article in the same journal described a case of severe liver damage caused by treating psoriasis with one of the drugs which doctors use.

There seems to be a close association between psoriasis, arthritis and diabetes, as well as other disorders of blood sugar regulation, such as hypoglycemia. Along with an inherited tendency toward arthritis and diabetes, certain eating habits handed down from one generation to another seem to suggest that diets in which sugar plays too big a part may be involved in all these disorders. It's a simple thing to eliminate sugar in all forms from one's meals and see whether the psoriasis clears up. It's always wise to consider white sugar as a harmful drug and treat it as such. Just avoid it as you would a poison.

Several years ago some skin specialists got excited over the possibility that psoriasis might be caused by trouble with one of the amino acids, tryptophane. No one knows why, but apparently some psoriatics improve when this one amino acid is almost entirely removed from their diets. Mealtimes become somewhat monotonous, since the single high-protein food which contains no tryptophane is turkey. Most other foods contain it.

Two New York physicians, Dr. Harry Spiera and Dr.

Albert M. Lefkovits, designed a low tryptophane diet which, they said, brought great improvement to a number of patients. One 19-year-old woman with psoriasis patches on face, chest, abdomen, arms and legs took the usual hospital diet for one week, then was placed on the low-tryptophane diet. Her skin cleared in one week. Two weeks later she had no skin symptoms.

Another patient, a 46-year-old woman, had suffered from psoriasis for 17 years when she was put on the "turkey diet." Her psoriasis symptoms were relieved and scalp hair started to grow for the first time in 10 years. Whenever she goes off the "turkey diet," her psoriasis symptoms recur.

The point is not to add turkey to your usual diet. Turkey must become the main source of protein in your diet and it must be eaten every day at almost every meal. A typical day's diet outlined in *Medical World News* for October 13, 1967 recommends a breakfast of nothing but orange juice and coffee with heavy cream; lunch consists of grapefruit juice, steamed white meat of turkey, boiled potato, stewed tomatoes, pears, heavy cream, coffee and butter for cooking. Dinner is tomato juice, steamed white meat of turkey, boiled potato, butter, canned asparagus, grapefruit and coffee with heavy cream. In all cases the doctors gave niacin (vitamin B3), which is closely connected with the amino acid tryptophane and which must be taken if tryptophane is not in the diet, or the deficiency disease pellagra will result.

We have heard nothing about the turkey diet for several years, so we do not know whether it is still being prescribed. The diet outlined above is so low in protein and high in fat that it would seem quite dangerous to undertake it on one's own, without a doctor's supervision. It seems to us a far better idea might be to reconstruct one's diet along generally healthful lines and use as much white meat of turkey as possible in the diet, just to avoid the tryptophane in other poultry and meat. Turkey is one of the least expensive foods you can buy at present, so it should not be difficult to substitute it for meat and other poultry items.

Finally, we found a note indicating that levels of the trace mineral zinc are low in victims of psoriasis. The *Lancet* for November 11, 1967 reported on tests made of patients with psoriasis and those with leg ulcers and other skin diseases. The level of zinc in the blood of psoriatics and other skin patients was low. The British writers tell us that zinc deficiency in animals results in a condition like psoriasis. Modern diets, high in refined sugar and starch, invite zinc deficiency.

CHAPTER 11

Some Unusual Aspects of Low Blood Sugar

RECENTLY GREAT INTEREST has been aroused in a new dietetic treatment for multiple sclerosis. It was introduced by a famous British writer, Roger MacDougall, who has MS himself. Mr. MacDougall's disease had progressed to the point where he could barely move or speak when he began to work out a diet program on which, over the years, he brought about complete remission of all his symptoms. He is now well and will remain so as long as he sticks with his diet.

Sugar is all but prohibited on the diet, which has several other important recommendations. Our interest in MacDougall's diet was sparked by the fact that, for years, a number of very knowledgeable researchers have theorized that MS may be the result of low blood sugar. In June, 1966 *The Journal of the American Geriatrics Society* published an article by Dr. S.J. Roberts, who presented what he called a "unitarian hypothesis" on the cause and treatment of multiple sclerosis.

He believes, he says, that MS is brought about by injury to the nervous system caused by low blood sugar, combined with other symptoms like water retention or edema. Young people—especially those with diabetic relatives—suffering from long-standing hypoglycemia who also have recurrent edema or swelling, plus severe vascular headaches, may also have symptoms of narcolepsy (a tendency to sudden overwhelming daytime sleepiness), plus the nerve symptoms of MS. Such patients, says Dr. Roberts, should be considered to be in a pre-MS state. By diagnosing this correctly, the doctor can prescribe a diet to prevent a full-blown case of MS.

Dr. Roberts studied 13 MS patients and 60 MS-prone patients. He found that 69 per cent of the MS patients and 65 per cent of the MS-prone patients suffered from low blood sugar which afflicted them only in the afternoon, not in the morning. These patients' secretion of insulin increased during the day, so that they should have food at shorter and shorter intervals as the day progresses—perhaps every two hours by late afternoon.

In addition to the usual diet for treating low blood sugar, Dr. Roberts stresses the importance of these measures:

1. Excessive smoking and caffeine-intake should be curtailed. Both habits can aggravate low blood sugar symptoms.

2. Alcohol should be avoided since it can reduce the output of glucose by the liver, which may precipitate or exaggerate low blood sugar.

3. Excessive fluid with meals and hurried eating should be avoided.

4. Adequate rest and avoidance of undue physical exhaustion and emotional tension are desirable. The return of energy which comes after the low blood sugar condition improves sometimes causes these patients to put on intensive bursts of work or activity which exhausts them. Dr. Roberts then suggests drugs which the doctor can give to hasten the improvement.

In a 1963 letter to the editor of *The New England Journal of Medicine*, Dr. Roberts states that he has investigated migraine headache and also so-called histamine headache and believes that both are caused by low blood sugar. Histamine headaches occur in early morning, which is the time when low blood sugar is most common. It can be prevented by abstaining from sugar and sugary foods before bedtime and in early morning hours. He thinks that allergic reactions to chocolate are not caused by the chocolate itself, but by the large amounts of sugar which chocolate contains.

An article in *Metabolism*, October, 1968, describes the effects of coffee on blood sugar. Volunteers were tested with a sugar solution or with a sugar solution plus coffee. Those who had both sugar and coffee developed lower blood sugar levels after meals than those who had just sugar. And the level of the fats in the blood of those who had sugar and coffee was higher than in those who had just sugar. So it seems that people who drink coffee with sugar in it may be greatly increasing the potential for trouble where blood sugar levels are concerned.

Nutrition Reviews for July, 1968 reported on experiments which showed that laboratory rats who were made deficient in the trace mineral manganese suffered from defective mechanism for regulating blood sugar. Restoring plenty of manganese to the diet brought the regulatory mechanism back to normal. The article reminds us that chromium, another trace mineral, is also related to the body's ability to produce just the right amount of insulin to regulate blood sugar properly.

Wholewheat flours contain 46 parts per million of manganese, while white flours contain only about 6.5 parts per million. About the same is true of chromium. All the trace minerals in sugarcane are removed when white sugar is made, so any amount of white sugar puts a burden on the body mechanism for dealing with sugar, since the relevant trace minerals are not present. The healthy rats in the experiment described above were getting 125 parts per million of manganese. We are told that human beings, eating diets in which sugar and refined carbohydrates are abundant while fruits and vegetables are slighted, might be getting as little as 5 parts per million of manganese.

Medical Tribune for December 11, 1969 presented the

view of a world-famous expert in diabetes who said, "there is no evidence today that a high blood sugar—past 150-200—is harmful. There is overwhelming evidence that a blood sugar below 100, below 60 or 70 . . . is very harmful."

According to an article in the August 21, 1970 *New York Times*, Princess Margaret of England suffers from intense migraine headaches. She is also a chain-smoker and has great trouble fighting overweight. Doesn't all this suggest low blood sugar, brought on by too many sweets, which also produce the overweight tendency? Smoking, like sweets, gives brief respite from unpleasant low blood sugar symptoms, but, in the long run, creates more and more problems of blood sugar regulation.

For more information on Roger MacDougall's diet for treating multiple sclerosis, write to him at: Regenics, Ltd., 450 Edgware Road, London W2 1EG, England.

CHAPTER 12

Who Says You Don't Eat Sugar?

THE MAY, 1971 issue of *Today's Health*, replying to a query about low blood sugar, says that this disorder is caused by "drug intoxications, liver and intestinal disorders, and primary hormonal disturbances, involving the pituitary, adrenal and pancreas glands...A condition known as 'functional hypoglycemia' is caused by consuming a diet rich in sweets and starches. Excess carbohydrate in such a diet causes the pancreas gland to overact and lower the blood sugar within a few hours after a meal....

"Treatment for functional hypoglycemia is a high-protein diet containing less carbohydrate. It is true that protein also is broken down into sugar. But this occurs more slowly than in the case of starches, so that variations in blood sugar are not as drastic," *Today's Health* says.

So a diet rich in sweets and starches can cause one form of hypoglycemia? But you don't eat sugar, you say! You mean you don't add sugar to your coffee or tea; you don't spread it over your cereal and you don't eat it by the cube. But did you ever consider the amount of sugar that goes into many foods which you and your family may eat every day?

For example, candy may be 75-85 per cent sugar. Candy bars weighing one to five ounces contain 5 to 20 teaspoons of sugar. And look at these figures!

Angel cake or sponge cake, 1 piece, 6 teaspoons sugar.

Chocolate cake (2-layer icing), 1 piece, 15 teaspoons sugar.

Apple pie, 1 piece, 12 teaspoons sugar.

Cherry pie, 1 piece, 14 teaspoons sugar.

Custard or coconut pie, 1 piece, 10 teaspoons sugar.

Pumpkin pie, 1 piece, 10 teaspoons sugar.

Gingersnaps, 1 piece, 1 teaspoon sugar.

Molasses cookies, 3½-in. diameter, 2 teaspoons sugar.

Brownies, average, 3 teaspoons sugar.

Doughnuts, plain, 1 average, 4 teaspoons sugar.

Cream puffs, iced, 1 average, 5 teaspoons sugar.

Custard, baked, ½ cup, 4 teaspoons sugar.

Gelatin (the flavored kind), ½ cup, 4 teaspoons sugar.

Jam, 1 tablespoon, 3 teaspoons sugar.

Marmalade, 1 tablespoon, 3 teaspoons sugar.

Chocolate fudge, 1½-in. square, 4 teaspoons sugar.

Chewing gum, 1 stick, ½ teaspoon sugar.

Hard candy, 1 piece, ⅓ teaspoon sugar.

Marshmallow, 1 average, 1½ teaspoons sugar.

Ice cream, 1 cone or bar, 5 to 6 teaspoons sugar.

Chocolate milk, 1 cup, 6 teaspoons sugar.

Sweet cider, 6-oz. glass, 4½ teaspoons sugar.

Soft drinks, 6-oz. bottle, 4 teaspoons sugar.

Fruit cocktail, ½ cup, scant, 5 teaspoons sugar.

This information comes from a pamphlet published by the Dental Public Health Committee of the Academy of Dentistry, Toronto, Canada.

"Nutrition surveys have shown that many children have too generous amounts of pie, cake, candy and other sweet foods. There is evidence that the excessive use of sweet foods helps promote tooth decay. Bacteria present in the mouth form acid from sugar. The acid attacks tooth surfaces," the pamphlet states.

"It is common knowledge that sweet foods dull the appetite," the pamphlet continues. "A child may not eat enough protective foods to meet his requirements if he is allowed free rein among the sweets. Sweet foods are not cheap when food value is concerned, in many cases they provide only calories. They do not usually contain vitamins and minerals in the quantities found in the protective foods that are necessary for growth and health. . . .

"The use of nuts, popcorn, cheese, milk, vegetables, whole grain cereals, meat, eggs or unsweetened fruit instead of foods of higher sugar content is advisable. The in-between meal use of candy, gum, cookies, cake and soft drinks is particularly injurious to teeth."

And, as we have seen in this book, sweets can contribute to low blood sugar, diabetes, overweight, etc. As long ago as 1865 a fat man named William Banting put himself on a low-carbohydrate, high-protein diet and lost a pound a week for 38 weeks. He also lost most of the symptoms of ill health that had bothered him for years. Experimenting with his diet later, he discovered that, by adding only one ounce of sugar to his diet every day and making no other changes, he would gain one pound a week regularly. One ounce of sugar is about two tablespoons. Two cups of chocolate milk a day, a single piece of cake or pie, a couple of soft drinks or even a very small candy bar, with no other change in your diet, can burden you with 52 pounds of overweight at the end of a year! This might well put you on the road to hypoglycemia or diabetes.

CHAPTER 13

Brewers Yeast, Chromium and Your Blood Sugar

NEW RESEARCH IS turning up exciting prospects for using the trace mineral chromium in conjunction with brewers yeast to stabilize the wild blood sugar swings of diabetics and, presumably, victims of low blood sugar as well. Dr. Richard J. Doisy, a biochemist at the State University of New York Upstate Medical School Center in Syracuse, believes it is likely that "public health measures to ensure adequate chromium intake will be not only desirable but essential for the long-range health of this nation."

It seems that chromium, which is essential to human beings in very small or "trace" amounts, may soon be used to prevent and to treat the diabetes so common among older Americans and possibly also the raised levels of fats in their blood. It is believed that lack of enough insulin may be responsible for the accumulation of these fats. And, if chromium can be used to potentiate—that is, to make more powerful—the available insulin, then perhaps the fatty accumulations can be prevented.

Dr. Doisy has been testing elderly Americans for their chromium content. He found that they have far less chromium in their bodies than people of a like age in the

Middle East, the Far East and in more primitive nations in Africa. And, along with the lack of chromium goes the impairment of blood sugar regulating machinery which is controlled by insulin. Dr. Doisy and his colleagues have found that lack of chromium is not confined to the elderly people. Even among much younger patients, Dr. Doisy found that giving chromium improved "glucose tolerance" as well as lowering the blood levels of cholesterol and other fats.

Dr. Kenneth M. Hambidge of the University of Colorado Medical Center used hair samples to chart the blood levels of chromium in people of various ages. He found, according to *Medical World News* for October 11, 1974, that, after the first few months of life, babies showed a drop in the level of chromium in their blood. Women having babies had much less chromium in their blood after the child was born. Dr. Hambidge found that Americans of all ages are not getting enough chromium.

Dr. Doisy studied elderly people living in a housing project in Syracuse. Of 31 active, healthy people over 63, almost half had disorders of glucose tolerance—that is, impairment of their body's ability to deal successfully with sugary and starchy foods. Twelve of these people agreed to take brewers yeast. Within a month, half of them had normal glucose tolerance. Their cholesterol levels also dropped from an average of 245 milligrams to 205 milligrams.

Of course, brewers yeast contains another substance which is known to reduce cholesterol levels—vitamin B3 (niacin). But for this you need large amounts of niacin. Dr. Doisy believes his volunteers were not getting enough of this vitamin from the yeast supplement to be responsible for the abrupt drop in cholesterol. It must be the chromium along with a factor which is found in brewers yeast called Glucose Tolerance Factor (GTF), which seems to make the chromium more available to the body.

Children apparently can use chromium much more successfully than older folks. The older folks did not

B Vitamins in One Gram of Brewers Yeast
(One Gram Is Less Than Half a Teaspoon)

Vitamin B1 (Thiamine)	150 micrograms
Vitamin B2 (Riboflavin)	50 micrograms
Vitamin B3 (Niacin)	400 micrograms
Vitamin B6 (Pyridoxine)	40 micrograms
Pantothenic acid	100 micrograms
Biotin	1.25 micrograms
Choline	3,350 micrograms
Inositol	4,425 micrograms
Folic acid	5 micrograms

respond to chromium for several months. But when they took the GTF factor in yeast along with the chromium they responded within a month. So it seems that the ability of the body to convert chromium into a usable substance declines with age. Some of Dr. Doisy's diabetic patients have reported that the GTF in brewers yeast has stabilized their blood sugar levels and has prevented attacks of low blood sugar which, in a diabetic, can be very serious.

Dr. Doisy found that giving his patients large amounts of sugar brought about excessive excretion of chromium. Such a finding reveals that white refined sugar can damage the susceptible person in two ways, with regard to blood sugar levels. First, practically all the chromium that is present in sugar cane is removed when the sugar is refined. So the person who eats white sugar must somehow deal with it, without the help of the chromium which accompanies it in the natural form of sugar cane. Now we discover that eating white sugar alone causes the body to excrete whatever chromium it has, which makes the situation far, far worse. No wonder so many Americans are deficient in chromium when so large a part of their diet is white sugar and foods that contain it.

A new publication of the National Academy of

Sciences, *Geochemistry and the Environment, Volume 1, the Relation of Selected Trace Elements to Health and Disease*, throws additional light on the chromium deficiency problem. Dr. Walter Mertz, a physician-nutritionist of the U.S. Agricultural Research Service, wrote the chapter on chromium in collaboration with a committee of other experts. He tells us that a certain form of chromium—trivalent chromium—was discovered in 1959 to be required by the body to manufacture the glucose tolerance factor which regulates blood sugar. When an individual is not getting enough chromium he suffers from what doctors call "impaired glucose tolerance" and the amount of insulin available for his body is reduced.

"Under special conditions," says Dr. Mertz, "chromium deficiency can result in impaired growth, retardation, fasting hyperglycemia and glycosuria (sugar in the urine), which is a definite symptom of diabetes. Chromium deficient rats develop fatty plaques in their heart arteries, as well as high levels of cholesterol in their blood. Such symptoms can be controlled by giving the animals chromium. There seems to be little danger of getting too much. Animals have been given as much as 100 parts per million in their food without any ill effects, although another chemical form of chromium—the hexavalent form—is toxic."

Studying soils in this country, geologists found that the amount of chromium they contain varies widely from place to place. They could not pinpoint any relationship between localities where there was little chromium and incidence of diabetes, but this might be expected since so many foods are shipped in from other localities. Some soils contain as little as 1 part per million of chromium, others as much as 3,000 parts per million. So it's possible that food raised in one locale may contain much more chromium than that raised in some other area.

In *Trace Elements in Human and Animal Nutrition*, Dr. E. J. Underwood says that foods which are rich in the GTF, as brewers yeast is, are of special importance because every unit of chromium which they contain is better used by the body than is the chromium found in other foods which do not have the GTF. Dr. Underwood tells us that a sample of wholewheat was found to contain 1.7 parts per million (ppm) of chromium, a sample of white flour contained 0.23 ppm, and a sample of white bread contained 0.14 ppm. A whole nation brought up on white bread, along with hundreds of other foods made of white flour and white sugar should be expected to be short on chromium.

Dr. Mertz tells us that the ability of the body to use chromium depends to a large extent on the form in which the chromium exists. Animals, as well as human beings, have a limited ability to make over inorganic chromium which they eat into the GTF. And they do this apparently in the intestine. Like so many other important functions, this work is carried out by the intestinal bacteria that inhabit this part of us. This suggests that we do everything possible to create a perfectly functioning colon where healthful bacteria can live. And that suggests the use of yogurt, buttermilk and other foods which contain the *lactobacillus* bacteria which preserve the health of the colon. Indeed, lack of this factor may be one reason why digestive disorders are so frequently linked with diabetes and other conditions of disordered blood sugar regulation.

Dr. Mertz believes that the adult human requirement for chromium may turn out to be between 10 and 30 milligrams daily. Dr. Henry Schroeder, a pioneer and a worldwide authority on trace minerals, believes that using stainless steel cooking utensils may be valuable in our quest for more chromium. Perhaps, he says, some small amount of chromium may leach out of the stainless steel into the food and prove to be beneficial.

"Glucose tolerance in man declines with age, and a large proportion of elderly Americans have abnormal glucose tolerance tests and tissue chromium levels in the United States also decline with age," says Dr. Mertz. "Repeated pregnancies, as well as diabetes, are associated with decreased tissue chromium levels. Higher intake of refined sugars, which furnish almost no chromium, results in a significantly increased urinary chromium excretion and can lead to overall negative chromium balance. All these factors suggest that part of our population may be in a state of marginal chromium deficiency."

There is no need to wait until federal health authorities decide to set daily recommendations for chromium and then decide to enrich all sugar and flour with chromium— if, indeed, they ever get around to doing such a thing. It is obvious that our nation-wide lack of chromium is due to the refined and processed foods we eat every day. So cross them off your list of acceptable foods.

Eat only whole foods: whole grains, whole cereals, wholegrain breads, muffins and crackers. Eat no white sugar or any food that contains it. Shop for fresh foods only: meat, poultry, fish, eggs, dairy products, fresh fruits and vegetables. Get as many of these as you can from your health food store. And depend on your health food store entirely for those staples which are guaranteed to be whole foods—cereals, flours or breads, nuts, seeds, beans, peas,

Debittered Brewers Yeast (Approximate Analysis)	
Protein	50%
Carbohydrate	31%
Fat	5.8%
Calories per gram	3.5
Calcium	0.125%
Phosphorus	1.5%
Potassium	1.62%
Magnesium	0.25%
Sodium	0.22%
Copper	8.5 ppm.
Iron	55 ppm.
Zinc	45 ppm.
Manganese	6.5 ppm.

soybeans, etc.

And buy some brewers yeast today. Start to use it in everything you prepare where it is appropriate: All baked foods, meat loaves, casseroles, hot cereals, salads, blender drinks. Even in small amounts its store of nutrients is noteworthy.

As for chromium, it is available in small amounts in some multi-mineral formulas at your health food store. Why not bring this research to the attention of your physician, and perhaps he can locate other sources of chromium for you?

CHAPTER 14

The Importance of Zinc

UNLIKE CHROMIUM, zinc is a trace mineral which was only recently listed by the National Academy of Sciences as an essential mineral. Officially, adults need some 15 milligrams per day. Of course, health seekers and many researchers in this field of nutrition have been talking about zinc for many years and theorizing on its importance to human health.

For example, we have definite knowledge that zinc is closely tied in with the body's use of insulin. Zinc is plentiful in the pancreas where insulin is manufactured. This suggests that the mineral may be lacking in people who suffer from low blood sugar and/or diabetes.

We know, too, that zinc is concentrated in the male sex organs, especially the prostate gland in which sperm is stored. Disorders of this gland are now so commonplace as to be almost an epidemic among Western men. The gland swells and cuts off the urinary flow, resulting in a painful, disabling condition which may progress to cancer.

We know also that zinc is essential for healing. Some researchers believe lack of zinc may be part of the reason for our epidemic of hardening of the arteries. Dr. Carl C. Pfeiffer of the New Jersey Neuropsychiatric Institute believes that lack of zinc and manganese may be one of the many causes of schizophrenia. Getting plenty of zinc may help the body to withstand the onslaught of certain cancer-producing chemicals.

In his new book, *The Best Health Ideas I Know*, Robert Rodale, son of the late J. I. Rodale, says there is lots of evidence that we need far more zinc than the present estimate for a daily allowance. One of the main reasons may be that the zinc content of our food is declining all the time because of the use of modern commercial fertilizers which provide no zinc. Yields on grain are increasing because of all the fertilizer our farmers use, but the zinc content of soils is dropping, not only in this country but also in many other parts of the world.

He tells us that a group of Colorado children were recently found to be quite short on zinc, as indicated by slow growth rates and severe deficiencies in the senses of taste and smell. Another specialist in the field points out that vegetarians may suffer most from zinc deficiency. This mineral is needed for the body to use protein. It is most abundant in high protein foods like meat and fish. So vegetarians who use no animal products may lack zinc, even though they get enough protein in their vegetarian foods. They cannot use all this protein without enough zinc to process it. And vegetarian foods may be especially lacking in zinc due to lack in the soils in which food is grown.

Two Midwestern scientists, Dr. Donald F. Caldwell and Dr. Donald Oberleas, believe that as many as 80 per cent of all Americans may be deficient in zinc. Our bodies lose zinc in excretions when we have colds, also in perspiration. Zinc is lost, too, when foods are processed. Even canning and cooking cause some loss of the mineral. But most important is the amount lost when cereal foods and sugar are refined and made into white flour, processed cereals and white sugar.

In *Trace Elements and Man*, Dr. Henry Schroeder of Dartmouth states that refined white sugar contains 0.54 ppm of zinc; raw brown sugar contains 1.62 ppm of zinc; molasses contains 8.28 ppm of zinc.

"Refining of raw cane sugar into white sugar removes

most (93 per cent) of the ash, and with it go the trace elements necessary for metabolism of sugar: 93 per cent of the chromium, 89 per cent of the manganese, 98 per cent of the cobalt, 83 per cent of the copper, 98 per cent of the zinc and 98 per cent of the magnesium. These essential elements are in the residue molasses, which is fed to cattle," Dr. Schroeder states.

"For ourselves," he adds, "we avoid the refined flours and all sugar-containing foods, using wholewheat, brown rice (which also loses elements in being polished white), dark brown sugar with a high ash content, and all the natural sugars: corn, maple, honey, fruit juice, etc. Much 'raw' sugar imported into this country is considerably refined, because of excise taxes, and sugar with a high ash content is difficult to find. Brown sugar sticky from molasses is suitable; any sugar which flows freely is probably partly refined, regardless of color."

Dr. William Strain and Dr. Walter Pories are two scientists working constantly on zinc studies. They have found that the trace mineral helps to heal wounds, decreases pains in the legs of people suffering from intermittent claudication, a circulatory ailment, and possibly helps to prevent hardening of the arteries. According to Dr. Jean Mayer of Harvard, zinc also helps you to recover from fatigue caused by exercise and helps undo the effects of alcohol.

Two Tennessee doctors reported rapid healing of gums after tooth extraction when zinc was given. More than 30 different enzyme systems in the body depend on zinc as one of their ingredients—about three times more than are dependent on magnesium. Enzyme systems are those groups of nutrients—proteins, hormones, vitamins and minerals—which bring about chemical changes in our bodies, allowing us to utilize food and build it into our cells or use it as energy.

One specialist in zinc metabolism believes adults should be getting up to 25 milligrams daily. Dr. Harold Rosenberg, in *The Doctor's Book of Vitamin Therapy*, recommends up to 30 milligrams. Supplements of higher potency are available only on prescription. These are generally zinc sulfate, zinc gluconate, zinc chloride. Zinc carbonate, which seems most acceptable, since it is a natural product which is mined, is apparently not yet available as a supplement for human beings, although it is used in animal feed. Bone meal contains zinc in natural form, but not a great deal in terms of the potencies we are talking about above.

Fish and shellfish contain more zinc than any other foods. Oysters are abundant sources. Liver, beef, egg yolk, brewers yeast are other good sources. And, of course, there are zinc supplements at your health food store, either in individual potencies or in one-a-day formulas.

CHAPTER 15

One Cause of Migraine Headaches

"THERE IS A TREE. For a minute we won't give the tree a name. Its branches are called Diabetes, Heart Disease, Overweight, Low Blood Sugar, Peptic Ulcer, Migraine, Allergy, and half a dozen other diseases that are so common nowadays. The name of the tree might be, A Disturbed Way of Handling Carbohydrates," writes Dr. Robert C. Atkins in *Dr. Atkins' Diet Revolution*.

Migraine headaches, one of these branches, have possibly been the subject of more medical and psychiatric investigation than any other common health disorder. Predictably, it has occurred to very few in the medical profession to study the kind of food eaten by the typical migraine sufferer—or the kind of food that should be eaten and is not. Most doctors seem to regard diet as something irrelevant to good health, or, for that matter, poor health.

A migraine headache is unlike any other experience in the world. The agonizing pain, which may throb for hours or days, is accompanied by nausea, vomiting, discomfort in light, and sometimes diarrhea. The sufferer can find no relief. Drugs which may alleviate the pain temporarily never completely cure the condition.

Two London physicians tell, in the *British Medical Journal* for November 19, 1966, how they brought on migraine headaches in six out of 12 chronic migraine victims by simply withholding food from 10 o'clock one evening until 5 o'clock the next evening. During this time they made careful note of the blood sugar levels of these volunteers. They think their results show that migraine in some individuals is triggered by low blood sugar caused by missing a meal or several meals.

What were the symptoms of these induced headaches? The same symptoms the patient had always experienced during his attacks: headache or sometimes a dull ache or unpleasant feeling in the head, nausea, a feeling of coldness, sweating, hunger, and lack of the ability to concentrate.

Say the authors, "We believe some patients have some of their attacks fired off by persistent hypoglycemia."

About 23 years ago a remarkable book published in the United States was saying the same thing and was relating low blood sugar not only to migraine but to many even more serious disorders—alcoholism, allergy, multiple sclerosis, epilepsy. *Body, Mind and Sugar*, by E. M. Abrahamson and A. W. Pezet told of alleviation and complete cures of all these disorders by the simple expedient of following a diet which does not allow the blood sugar to fall below normal levels. It is the same high-protein, low-carbohydrate diet that we have mentioned throughout this book.

The diet is sensible and simple enough for any of us to follow. But it is mandatory for the individual with low blood sugar. One of the most important elements of this diet, as we have said, is the frequency of meals. You must eat as often as specified. If you are going to be some place where food is unobtainable, take it with you: nuts, high-protein wafers from the health food store, sunflower seeds, cheese, fruit.

If you know someone who suffers from migraine headaches, why not tell him about this diet? You may save his health, his happiness, perhaps even his sanity.

CHAPTER 16

Vitamin Therapy for the Hyperactive Child

"SHAMBLES HAVE BEEN MADE out of the FDA's Minimum Daily Requirements and Recommended Daily Allowances of various vitamins and minerals by countless scientific studies," states Dr. George P. Prastka of Costa Mesa, California. "This is because there is a tremendous variation in the range of the requirements of the so-called 'normal' person. Indeed, we have yet to discover the optimum amount of these substances for the human body. This is even more true of the individual. One person may require perhaps 1,000 times more of a given nutrient than another, due in many cases to problems he may have in assimilating it."

In working with Schizophrenics Anonymous, Chapter 30, in Eastchester, New York, Elizabeth A. Plante, R.N., says that "these acute cases are due to either a lifelong deprivation of essential vitamins, such as C, B3, B1, B6 and E, or to a personal, genetic need for higher than average quantities of these vitamins, or both."

"Our research work...shows that food alone cannot supply the indispensable nutritional elements," reports Dr. W. D. Currier of Pasadena, California. "Vitamins and other supplements are urgently needed. No one, no group of doctors knows how much of these supplements is needed, especially in severe cases of malnutrition. The so-called RDA has no meaning in most physical and mental illness. Thus, I frequently prescribe huge amounts of nutritional supplementation, relying upon computerized laboratory analysis and other data as well as my own clinical evaluation."

Today, there is a growing recognition that the hyperactive "problem" child, the child with a learning disability, may, indeed, be suffering from a physical disorder related chiefly to nutrition and the possibly very high nutritional requirements of some of these children. This is the viewpoint of Dr. Allan Cott, a New York psychiatrist.

Dr. Cott enlarges on his theory in an article in *Schizophrenia*, Vol. 3, No. 2. The title of the article is "Orthomolecular Approach to the Treatment of Learning Disabilities." The word "orthomolecular" was first used by Dr. Linus Pauling several years ago, when he proposed a world-shaking theory which, greatly simplified, theorizes that mental illness is caused by malnutrition of parts of the brain and nervous system. The victim may not appear to be suffering from malnutrition; he may have no other symptoms of vitamin and mineral deficiency.

Dr. Cott and many psychiatrists and physicians across the United States and Canada are using massive doses of a number of vitamins in the belief that these patients have extra large requirements for these vitamins. Many of these specialists prescribe a useful diet as well.

Dr. Cott tells us that, in the last five years, he has treated 500 children with this approach and has had better results than he has had with any other kind of treatment. He says there are very few cases of dramatic response by disturbed children treated with the usual drugs. He believes in using megadoses of a number of vitamins—not just one or two. He says that up to 1,000 times the usual vitamin doses may be required. He has successfully treated adults with massive doses of vitamin B3 (niacin), vitamin B6 (pyridoxine), vitamin C, vitamin E and others. He has had remarkable results in treating schizophrenia. So he began treatment of schizophrenia and autistic children and "found improvement in many of these children to be more dramatic than in adults." He tells us that the treatment is most effective if it is given to difficult children when they are quite young. As they grow older, longer and longer treatment is needed.

Dr. Cott's descriptions of these unfortunate children are arresting. He says that in most instances within three to six months the child begins to understand and obey commands. He shows a willingness to cooperate with parents and teachers. The hyperactivity which is one of the main symptoms of the childhood mental troubles begins to subside.

The children brought to him have been exposed to "every form of treatment and every known tranquilizer and sedative with little or no success, even in controlling the hyperactivity." After treatment with massive vitamin therapy, those who have never spoken begin to babble. Those who can already speak begin to show steady improvement in forming phrases and short sentences. "In their general behavior, they show a greater appreciation for the people in their environment. They become more loving and not only permit cuddling and hugging, but seek it. Bizarre food choices change slowly to include a large variety of foods."

Dr. Cott gives disturbed children and children with learning disabilities these vitamins: Niacin or niacinamide (another form of this B vitamin)—one to two grams daily, depending on weight. Vitamin C—one to two grams daily. Vitamin B6—200 to 400 milligrams daily. Calcium pantothenate (this is one form of the B vitamin pantothenic acid)—400-600 milligrams daily. These are starting doses for little ones weighing 35 pounds or more. He varies the dose depending on individual response.

In Russia, Dr. Cott reports, doctors are using vitamin B15 (pangamic acid) in cases of retardation. They believe it helps supply oxygen to brain tissues. This vitamin is not recognized officially in the United States.

Dr. Cott tells us of a brain-injured child who had had seizures every day for three years. Eleven days after he started on vitamin B6 therapy, he had his first day free from seizures. During all those years he had been taking the tranquilizers usually prescribed for this condition and the seizures had not stopped.

Another child, who had multiple daily seizures for two years, became free from seizures 72 hours after the massive doses of vitamins were begun. He was still well four years later. "I have seen very few cases of childhood schizophrenia, autism or brain injury in whom seizure activity did not respond to the megavitamins," says Dr. Cott.

The New York psychiatrist believes that hyperactivity in early childhood may be an indication that schizophrenia will occur later in life.

"The universal observations on the dietary habits of brain-injured children, hyperactive children, learning-disabled children and psychotic children have been that these children eat a diet which is high in cereals, in carbohydrate foods and those foods prepared with sugar," Dr. Cott states.

As might be expected, Dr. Cott has found an abnormally high incidence of low blood sugar, as well as its opposite, lack of enough insulin to handle carbohydrates properly. He has also found an abnormally high family history of diabetes in this group. In children who show disorders of blood sugar regulation, he has found disturbance of histamine levels and trace mineral levels as well. In 26 of 30 children he found lower than normal levels of several minerals in analyzing hair for mineral content. Lead was present in every sample tested.

Summing up his work and the work of others in treating mentally disturbed children—those who cannot speak, cannot learn, cannot control their hyperactivity—Dr. Cott says, "Investigation of this treatment modality by controlled studies should be given the highest priority, for we are dealing with a patient population of 20 million children."

Dr. Abram Hoffer is another psychiatrist who is using the megavitamin therapy approach to deal with hyperactive children. In the *Canadian Medical Journal* for July 22, 1972, he writes:

"I would like to present one case in order to illustrate the kind of results which might be expected. This young patient, aged 14, was first seen April 6, 1972. The chairman of the Pupil Services Department of the Board of Education stated that for the first three months of 1972 the patient did no work at school, was disruptive a good deal of the time, came to school late and left without permission and engaged in bizarre behavior, such as smearing blood all over his face from a small cut on his hand. He was not bad all the time but had many bad days and when he was bad he was apparently horrid.

"His behavior became so strange and bizarre that it was impossible to leave him alone," Dr. Hoffer continues. "His actions were summarized as being very impulsive and completely unpredictable, and he seemed never to learn anything. It was the conclusion of the teacher that there was something seriously wrong with this patient and that they could no longer deal with him at school. His I.Q. was around 80 but this was obviously much too low, because he seemed to be of normal intelligence.

"The patient's mother reported that he had been somewhat hyperactive most of his life but that he had become much worse over the past two years. He was referred to a child psychiatrist who, after several examinations, reported that he was normal and that he would grow out of his problem. However, he did not and he continued to present very difficult problems at school and began to develop behavior problems at home."

Dr. Hoffer goes on to describe some of the imaginary things bothering this child. The boy thought that people were "watching" him. He saw faces in the air. He heard his name being called when no one was calling him. He felt that he could hear his own thinking inside his head. He was sure that people were making fun of him and running him down, gossiping about him. In addition, the boy was extremely restless, irritable and cranky, and so hyperactive that on this score he stood within the range of schizophrenia, which is, of course, very serious.

Dr. Hoffer gave the child two B vitamins, niacinamide and pyridoxine—three grams of the former per day and ½ gram of the B6. These are massive doses. The official recommendation for a daily diet level of niacin is 20 mg. for a boy this age. The RDA for vitamin B6 is 2 milligrams.

The boy was to report back one month later. But he cancelled the appointment because he was working, selling ice cream. At the end of May he came to see Dr. Hoffer, reported that he felt better, was getting good grades in school, had no trouble getting along with the other children. He had received an excellent report from the teacher who had considered him almost hopeless.

"Since it is a general scientific rule that, where one patient will respond to a particular treatment, there must be others who will also do so, I suggest that all physicians try treating hyperkinetic (hyperactive) children with vitamins, which seem to be so effective in my hands," Dr. Hoffer says.

If you know a family in which there is a child suffering from any of these disorders—or an adult with schizophrenia—ask them to get in touch with the Huxley Institute for Biosocial Research, 1114 First Avenue, New York City; phone 212-759-9554. The Institute maintains literature and the names and addresses of physicians, psychiatrists and other professionals who use megavitamin therapy.

CHAPTER 17

Aggression and Low Blood Sugar

IN THE MARCH 17, 1975 issue of *The New York Times*, a number of doctors, psychoanalysts, sociologists, attorneys and others speculate on why there is a rising crime wave among juveniles in the United States. The article, "Violent Crime by Young People: No Easy Answer," was written by Enid Nemy.

These experts attribute the juvenile crime problem to:

1. The American dream and the country's emphasis on brawn, rather than brains.

2. The easy availability of guns and lack of a national gun law.

3. The disintegration of the family and the deterioration of discipline in schools.

4. The prevalence of violence in the media, particularly on TV and in films.

5. The lack of deterrents in the form of positive punishment.

6. Racial attitudes that neutralize guilt feelings.

Wayne Mucci, former director of the Bureau of Institutions and Facilities for New York City, notes that violence "is an accepted technique of getting something, with no sense of personal responsibility for actions." He indicates that he had seen research figures indicating that "children who watched TV had seen about 11,000 murders by the time they were 14 years old."

The *Times* article goes on to say that juvenile crime figures "reinforce the beliefs of some criminologists that lack of deterrents in the judicial system encourages young first offenders."

And Dr. Robert Martinson, who, with two colleagues, spent eight years looking into thousands of studies on correctional treatment, said his research had indicated that "rehabilitation doesn't have much effect, if any."

With all due respect to these learned criminologists, we believe they are barking up the wrong tree. It is true that the above-named six points are a contributing factor to juvenile delinquency. But this is an oversimplification of the real problem. We would suggest that many of these offending juveniles—as well as thousands of recalcitrant adults—are suffering from chronic nutritional deficiencies, which, together with the environmental factors enumerated above result in antisocial behavior. Among the reasons for our belief is that "rehabilitation doesn't have much effect."

In other words, if a person is suffering from pellagra or low blood sugar or some other nutritional problem, you are not likely to correct his behavior by throwing him in the clink and analyzing what kind of TV programs he watched or whether or not there was a deterioration of the discipline at his school. We are confident that nutrition and what the prisoner eats have never entered into these discussions.

Dr. El Kholy, an Egyptian physician, writing in the newsletter, *Schizophrenia*, believes that the lack of niacin (vitamin B3) may have a great deal to do with the personality of criminals. From 1941 to 1948, Dr. Kholy studied the relationship between crime and pellagra, the disease that is brought on by a niacin and protein deficiency. He maintains that pellagra can easily be mistaken for a schizophrenic personality.

Dr. Kholy examined 1,150 people who had been accused of violent crimes. And he found that 206 or 18 per cent had pellagra. They had been imprisoned for murder, threats to kill, attempted murder, serious assault, kidnapping, arson, rape and other crimes. Over one-third of all who were later declared to be insane murderers were found to have pellagra.

"... The psychiatrist finds an important parallel between pellagra and schizophrenia. Both conditions... are clinically so similar that they have been, and are, easily confused. Both respond to treatment with vitamin B3, although psychiatrists who have not used the megavitamin B3 approach still deny this, and both can be prevented by adequate intake of vitamin B3... As a rule patients who have recovered from schizophrenia and are well physically and mentally will not relapse while taking adequate doses of either nicotinic acid or nicotinamide," *Schizophrenia* reports.

"By analogy, if elimination of pellagra reduces crimes of violence, how much more will eradication of schizophrenia achieve? It is suggested, therefore, that perhaps the addition of nicotinamide (one form of B3) to our food in doses of one gram per day or more will do for schizophrenia what the fortification of flour with much smaller doses of nicotinamide has done for pellagra."

Dr. R. Glen Green of Canada is confident that many inmates in the penitentiary have what he calls "subclinical pellagra," and he thinks that they are incarcerated because they have this disorder.

"The meanest people in the world are probably the Qolla, an Andean subculture inhabiting the area around Lake Triticaca between Peru and Bolivia," writes Robert J. Trotter in the February 3, 1973 issue of *Science News*. "Anthropological literature has described the members of this group as the meanest and most unlikable people on earth—the classic example of an extreme personality type dominated by excessive hostility and aggressiveness. In recent years the Qolla have been called everything from anxious and fearful to dishonest and vindictive. But their rancor is hardly a recent discovery; it is almost legendary. In the 16th century a Mercedarian friar, Padre Martin de

Muru'a, described the Qolla as irrational, cruel, un-civilized, stupid and dull."

Mr. Trotter went on to discuss the work of Dr. Ralph Bolton of Pomona College, California, who, with his wife, spent five years living among the Qolla peasants and studying them. This research, which was later published in a book, was initially reported to us by Pomona College.

Dr. Bolton has found a connection between the abnormal behavior of these Peruvians and low blood sugar levels. This condition, as we have stated, can masquerade as many different physical diseases. Many of the unpleasant feelings that plague dieters on reducing diets low in protein (headaches, hunger, irritability, nervousness, etc.) may be associated with the low blood sugar condition such diets may produce. And the low blood sugar may be one reason why such diets are so hard to maintain.

The Qolla have no problems with reducing diets. Like poor people in our own country—especially those juveniles from the ghetto who get into trouble—they suffer gross dietary deficiencies from eating a low-protein, high-carbohydrate diet. In the case of the Qolla, their diet consists mostly of potatoes, barley, oats and quinoa, a grain which grows at high altitudes. In addition, they live in a hostile environment. The terrain is hilly, mountainous and barren. The climate is erratic, with hail, drought and frost, which means that harvests are likely to be uncertain and scanty.

Dr. Bolton describes the Qolla as people who enjoy a good fight, because "it makes one feel better." Very hostile and aggressive, these two million people are pretty regularly "spoiling for a fight" just for the heck of it. The anthropologist believes that the combination of circumstances—inadequate diet, overpopulation, scarcity of land, unpredictable weather and lack of enough oxygen (because of the altitude at which they live) may be the starting points for the development of low blood sugar levels.

He found the Qolla to be "strutting, swaggering

individuals," especially when they are drunk. They will go to outrageous lengths to insult others and precipitate a fight, sometimes indulging in monologues "describing their own ferocity while laughing at the puniness of their enemies." Threats produce such sensitivity in the Qolla that just the phrase "you'll see" can be construed as a verbal attack. Saying "I am a man" immediately implies that others are not men, so whoever is within hearing distance takes this sentence as an insult and a battle ensues.

Fighting and killing are not the only forms of aggression. Injuries, insults, stealing, rape, arson, abortion, slander, failure to pay debts, land ownership disputes and homicide are common. In one village of 1,200 Qolla, Dr. Bolton found that half of the heads of households had been involved, directly or indirectly, in homicide cases. The rate of homicide among the Qolla is 50 per 100,000—far higher than in almost any other group in the world.

Surprisingly, the traditional philosophy of the Qolla is far from aggressive. They believe in the Christian virtues of charity, compassion and cooperation with others. And they almost never perceive any discrepancy between their beliefs and their actions. Other anthropologists have always found the Qolla to be "the meanest and most unlikable people on earth." Traditionally this has been excused on the basis of the extreme hardness of their lives and the fact that they have usually lived under domination by one or another conquering nation.

Dr. Bolton believes this is not the complete story. Other nations living under harsh conditions do not have the same characteristics of aggression and hostility. True, the Qolla have been conquered many times, but, he says, they tend to ignore outside influences, even conquerors, and continue to go about their own hostile pursuits. They live in a constant state of anarchy.

The anthropologist had read about hypoglycemia and decided to test some of the Qolla. He did blood sugar analyses of all adult males in one village and found that blood sugar levels were low in 50 per cent of them.

Interestingly enough, they chew the coca leaf. *Encyclopedia Britannica* tells us that coca leaves are the substance from which cocaine is made. Their action is similar to that of opium, though somewhat less narcotic. They deaden the sense of taste and anesthetize the membranes of the stomach, thus cutting off hunger.

So it is possible, under the influence of coca, to go without food or consciousness of needing it for as long as three days. But the body starves, as might be expected. Continual heavy use of coca produces body wasting, mental failure, insomnia, circulatory weakness and dyspepsia. However, under the influence of the drug, addicts are able to perform great feats of endurance.

In addition to chewing coca leaves, the Qolla use a lot of alcohol, again, Dr. Bolton believes, in an effort to bring blood sugar levels up to a comfortable condition. Alcohol does this in susceptible persons, then causes these levels to drop far below normal, bringing on the same symptoms the alcoholic has tried to overcome. So it becomes necessary to have another and yet another drug of some kind, merely to keep going with any comfort.

Very little research has been done on low blood sugar in relation to aggression in recent years. But, during the 1940's a number of American doctors proposed the theory that low blood sugar is the leading cause of many acts of criminal violence—even murder.

Hypoglycemia may be a factor in some cases of criminal behavior in so-called "civilized" societies, says Dr. Bolton. An otherwise normal-appearing person may be driven to commit atrocities by his body's urge to restore a proper blood sugar balance. Aware that the body will go to extraordinary lengths to repair a malfunction within itself, Dr. Bolton believes that the Qolla are forced into aggressive behavior by their physical condition. He thinks that, through aggressive thought and activity, the Qolla unconsciously try to raise their blood sugar levels to a comfortable point. Psychologically they force themselves into a state of anger so their internal organs can temporarily restore a proper bodily balance.

Dr. Bolton believes that low blood sugar should be suspected when studying social conflict and behavior patterns of any "peasant" culture. We wonder why he specifies "peasant", since many of the circumstances he outlines appear to be just as prevalent on city streets, where badly nourished and desperate people commit crimes just to get money for drugs, where apparently sane people go berserk within hours of apparent sanity and kill wildly and indiscriminately anyone they can reach with a gun.

Dr. Bolton does not mention it, but obviously one form of stress on city streets must be the low blood sugar caused by a deficient diet overbalanced with sweets and carbohydrates, especially the concentrated sugar in soft drinks and candy. But he does say that his study opens up many research possibilities, for example, detailed studies of the relationship between coca chewing and other drug use and hypoglycemia; the relationship between alcohol consumption and hypoglycemia; and the consequences of hypoglycemia for other psychological processes such as perception, memory and cognition. He believes, too, that a study of aggressive societies and peaceful ones may lead eventually to a significant anthropological contribution to a general theory of human conflict and aggression.

CHAPTER 18

Coffee Is a No-No

DOCTORS CALL IT the "anxiety constellation." They meet it often and they may diagnose it as almost anything—usually psychiatric. The patient feels anxious, has insomnia, may complain of heart palpitations, light headedness, headache or inability to get his breath. Unless the doctor probes into the patient's daily life, he is not likely to guess that this patient may be suffering from "caffeinism." And if he looks even closer, he may find that his patient has hypoglycemia.

"Reports (in medical journals) are reasserting the significance of caffeine as a long recognized factor in the diagnosis of anxiety, because many doctors and patients do not recognize (the symptoms) for what they are. The patient overlooks the amount of caffeine he or she consumes every day in coffee, tea, cola drinks and over-the-counter medications," writes Lawrence K. Altman in the March 15, 1975 issue of *The New York Times*. His article is titled, "The Perils of Caffeine."

"As a result, the physician does not inquire about the patient's caffeine consumption. The doctor diagnoses an anxiety condition and prescribes tranquilizers instead of advising the patient to ration his caffeine consumption," Mr. Altman says.

The article quotes Dr. John F. Greden, who is studying the effects of caffeine on the body at the University of Michigan Medical Center in Ann Arbor. His initial findings are the outgrowth of research he did at Walter Reed Army Medical Center in Washington, D.C., and reported in the *American Journal of Psychiatry* in 1974.

"Dr. Greden reported that many Americans routinely ingest what pharmacologists consider large levels of caffeine, when they drink more than three cups of coffee a day," the *Times* states. "And when they take cola drinks, sip tea and swallow Excedrin, Anacin and other headache pills, they add to the cumulative dose... Pharmacologists consider doses greater than 250 milligrams as 'large.' Because caffeine affects all parts of the brain's cortex, the drug is capable of producing symptoms indistinguishable from anxiety, such as nervousness, irritability, agitation, trembling hands, muscle twitches and rapid breathing."

To give an idea of how much caffeine we may be ingesting daily from various sources, the *Times* reproduced a chart showing the approximate amounts of caffeine per unit:

1. *Beverages.* Brewed coffee (100 to 150 mg. per cup); instant coffee (86 to 99 mg. per cup); tea (60 to 75 mg. per cup); decaffeinated coffee (2 to 4 mg. per cup); cola drinks (40 to 60 mg. per glass).

2. *Prescription medications.* APC's (aspirin, phenacetin, caffeine) (32 mg. per tablet); Cafergot (100 mg. per tablet); Darvon compound (32 mg. per tablet); Fiorinal (40 mg. per tablet); Migral (50 mg. per tablet).

3. *Over-the-counter (OTC) analgesics.* Anacin, aspirin compound, Bromo Seltzer, Cope (32 mg. per tablet); Easy-Mens, Empirin compound, Midel, Vanquish (32 mg. per tablet); Excedrin (60 mg. per tablet); Pre-Mens (66 mg. per tablet).

4. *Many OTC cold preparations* (30 mg. per tablet).

5. *Many OTC stimulants* (100 mg. per tablet).

The Journal of the American Medical Association for September 16, 1974 relates the case of a young nurse married to a physician. For three weeks she had felt light-headed, tremulous, breathless. She had headaches and an irregular heartbeat. Her doctor referred her to a psychiatrist, certain that her trouble was fear that her husband might be sent to a war zone.

The nurse decided to do some diagnosing herself. She carefully analyzed everything she ate and drank all day and discovered that she was drinking exceptionally large amounts of coffee—10 to 12 cups a day. She had been making her coffee by a different method which she liked better, so she drank more. She went without coffee for three days and all her symptoms subsided. For two years she has had no more symptoms. Based upon the above chart, she might have been consuming as much as 1,800 milligrams of caffeine daily in coffee alone.

The above *Times* article records an experience related by Dr. Donald A. Molde of Reno, Nevada, who was writing in the *American Journal of Psychiatry*. One of Dr. Molde's patients, an inmate at the Nevada State Prison, had complained of severe anxiety symptoms, which Dr. Molde said had not responded to the usual treatment and drugs he had prescribed. It was later determined that the prisoner was drinking approximately 50 cups of coffee a day. He had a hot plate in his cell and, with a lot of time on his hands, he made coffee and drank it constantly.

"(The patient) substituted decaffeinated coffee, cutting his total coffee consumption by 60 per cent, and reported marked improvement in a very few days," Dr. Molde says.

A Florida physician reported (*JAMA*, October 25, 1971) on a patient who had retained fluid for 10 years. She suffered from swelling of hands, feet and ankles. In the evening she had trouble getting her shoes on and off. She drank an average of 8 to 10 cups of coffee daily. And she was always a "nervous wreck." She was told to switch to decaffeinated coffee. Within five days her edema (swelling) disappeared and never returned so long as she stayed with no-caf.

What coffee does to the fats in the blood has been studied for some time. Results seem to show that it increases fatty substances in the blood. In 1970, a New York physician reminded his fellow physicians in the

JAMA that caffeine also causes irregular heart rhythms. "It has always amazed me," he says, "that tea, coffee and occasionally cola drinks are consumed by patients in a coronary care unit, when so much other effort is directed by the medical and nursing staffs to the observation and control of arrythmias."

A career military officer came to a psychiatric outpatient clinic with a 2-year history of anxiety. He had dizziness, tremulousness, restlessness, frequent diarrhea, insomnia, and anxiety about his job. He had three complete physical examinations. The doctors could not discover what was the matter with him. He was given tranquilizers, which did not help but made him feel worse. Finally, he volunteered that he was drinking from 8 to 12 cups of coffee every day and often had cocoa at bedtime. He also had three or four cola drinks every day. The doctors told him he had been imbibing enormous amounts of caffeine and recommended that he stop drinking coffee and colas. As soon as he stopped, his symptoms began to disappear almost at once. He and the nurse mentioned above were given large doses of caffeine at a later date, and all the symptoms returned within a few days.

Says Dr. John F. Greden, whom we quote when he was at the Walter Reed Army Medical Center, "Many individuals complaining of anxiety will continue to receive substantial benefit from psycho-pharmacological agents (tranquilizers). For an undetermined number of others, subtracting one drug—caffeine—may be of greater benefit than adding another."

And, of course, caffeine has been related to diabetes and low blood sugar. Some researchers seem to show that coffee raises blood sugar. Some researchers seem to show that coffee raises blood sugar levels in the diabetic (who wants to keep them as low as possible) and drastically lowers blood sugar levels in victims of hypoglycemia. Dr. E. M. Abrahamson, in *Body, Mind and Sugar*, tells of patients who have completely stabilized their blood sugar levels by a high protein diet and no coffee, only to have violent low blood sugar reactions when they took as little as one cup of coffee.

What can you drink in place of coffee? Your health food store is brimming over with "coffee substitutes." First, there is decaffeinated coffee. This is made by treating coffee beans with a solvent which does not remain in the coffee. It removes nothing but the caffeine. Decaffeinated coffee tastes just as good as regular coffee. If you make it with a filter, it is impossible to tell the difference, except that it doesn't keep you awake, doesn't stimulate you, doesn't create fatty deposits, etc.

Coffee substitutes are usually made from cereals, ground and roasted so that they taste very much like coffee. Until you sample them and choose a favorite, don't decide that they just wouldn't appeal to you. Maybe they would.

Finally, there are the herb teas, over 100 varieties to choose from. The health seeker cherishes herb teas mostly for their pleasant aroma and taste and for the knowledge that they bring nothing harmful and may, in fact, contribute much in the way of trace minerals and other elements which are essential for good health. You can't go wrong with herb teas, which are certainly the best and most satisfying coffee substitutes of all.

CHAPTER 19

Don't Smoke!

CONCERNED ABOUT THE 3 per cent rise in cigarette smoking since 1973, the Federal Trade Commission has asked Congress for permission to require this more explicit warning on all packs: "Cigarette smoking is dangerous to health and may cause death from cancer, coronary heart disease, chronic bronchitis, pulmonary emphysema and other diseases."

Did you know that the smoke from one cigarette, even if not inhaled, exerts a tremendous influence on blood sugar level? A Swedish physician, writing in the October 30, 1965 issue of the *Lancet*, reports on experiments which were conducted in 1929 in Sweden. About 100 tests were done on 10 healthy volunteers who smoked cigarettes at varying intervals, so that their blood sugar could be measured before and at varying periods after each smoke.

In the case of one young woman who smoked four cigarettes in a morning, her blood sugar level rose from a healthy 97 or 99 to 111 or 114 and, finally, to 118 for the last cigarette smoked. The rise in this last case occurred in seven minutes. It represented an increase of 36 per cent.

The Swedish investigators also did tests on denicotinized cigarettes and found that they did not affect the blood sugar levels. However, cigars produced the same effect as cigarettes. So nicotine seems to be responsible.

Says the Swedish doctor who reported these tests, "Very few seem to be aware of this truly spectacular effect of smoking... The effect of the 'hunger cigarette' is easily explained by the rapid rise of blood sugar, which also explains the increased craving for tobacco in times of war and famine. The rapid fall of the blood sugar level after smoking throws further light on the habit of chain smoking—the craving for another pick-me-up...."

In other words, excessive and long-continued cigarette smoking may possibly result in such disorder of the blood sugar regulating mechanism as to produce diabetes or chronic low blood sugar. As we know, when blood sugar rises to disastrous heights within minutes, then plummets much too rapidly, it produces a sensation of hunger and possibly faintness. Now we are told that nicotine produces the same condition.

Many people who have tried to give up smoking complain that they immediately put on weight. They are trying, you see, to deal with a blood sugar mechanism already disordered by nicotine, so they eat whenever they would formerly have lit a cigarette. If these snacks are high protein foods, chances are that the nicotine addict, if he is not too far gone in addiction, can gradually bring his blood sugar levels back to normal and the craving for cigarettes will disappear completely and painlessly. But all too often the smoker is also a coffee, candy and soft drink addict as well. So even though he stops smoking, with a terrific effort of will power, he continues to eat candy, drink soft drinks and coffee and his blood sugar levels continue their wild swings from high to low, while his waistline steadily expands.

The answer for the person who wants to stop smoking is to omit everything that disorders blood sugar levels: cigarettes or cigars, coffee and any food containing large amounts of sugar. He should nibble frequently throughout the day on high-protein foods. It sounds incredible, but on this kind of diet the craving for nicotine, caffeine and sugar can be overcome completely within 10 days or two weeks.

"More people are attempting to give up cigarette

smoking, and some are receiving advice to replace this habit by eating mints and other similar sweets under the misapprehension that these are less injurious to teeth than chewing toffees," writes a doctor in the November 6, 1965 issue of the *Lancet.*

"Eighteen months ago," he continues, "a 20-year-old man who was dentally fit gave up cigarette smoking and began the habit of mint-sucking. He recently presented himself with over 50 carious lesions (decayed holes) in his teeth. X-rays taken 18 months ago and the recent examination confirmed this transformation. Many may not be aware of the devastation this particular kind of sweets can create in an otherwise healthy mouth."

The Journal of the American Medical Association for April 28, 1969 told of experiments in Canada which linked smoking to lack of vitamin C. Smoking apparently interferes with the body's ability to utilize the vitamin, according to Dr. Omer Pelletier, who conducted his experiments with the assistance of the Canadian Food and Drug Directorate.

By keeping his subjects on identical diets and giving them measured doses of the vitamin over a period of about three weeks, Dr. Pelletier found that:

1. Smokers have lower vitamin C levels than non-smokers.

2. It does not seem to matter how many cigarettes are smoked per day or how long the individual has been smoking. The vitamin level remains low. Three volunteers who had stopped smoking three to six months earlier had the same general blood levels of vitamin C as non-smokers, so their bodies had apparently repaired whatever mechanism it is that deals with vitamin C and cigarette smoke.

3. There was no sex difference. Women in both groups had the same blood levels of the vitamin as the men.

4. The test doses of vitamin C which were given at 8:30 in the morning were retained better than were those given at 4:30 in the afternoon. This seems to indicate that one

benefits more from vitamins if they are taken in the morning.

Although earlier experiments seemed to show that vitamin C is destroyed in the body of smokers (as it is in a test tube filled with smoke), so that smokers always need more than non-smokers, Dr. Pelletier believes his experiments show that the vitamin just is not used properly in the body of the smoker.

In any case, the lesson is the same for the health seeker. Smoking is for losers!

CHAPTER 20

Can Epilepsy Be Prevented by Diet?

THERE IS SOME evidence that epilepsy is related to blood sugar conditions. The book *Low Blood Sugar*, by Peter J. Steincrohn, M.D., answers the question of a patient who says, "My attacks of so-called *petit mal* epilepsy disappeared after the diagnosis and treatment of my low blood sugar. Is this possible?" Dr. Steincrohn answers, "Yes. There have been other instances in which hypoglycemia simulated epilepsy attacks."

He also relates low blood sugar conditions to a related condition, narcolepsy. This is a condition in which sleepiness prevails—but a sleepiness so intense that the patient simply cannot stay awake during the day, no matter how much sleep he has gotten the night before.

Says Steincrohn, "Only those who fight and struggle to stay awake during the day realize what it is to suffer and bear (at the same time) the taunts of those closest to them...Thus, over half a million Americans wear such false labels as sleepyhead, stupid, lazy because their families and friends (and their doctors) are unaware that they do indeed suffer from some medical disability and not from an imaginary illness. Many similar cases are helped by a low carbohydrate diet, high protein and administration of Ritalin or similar medication," says Dr. Steincrohn.

In their book *Body Mind and Sugar*, which introduced the subject of low blood sugar to the American people, E. M. Abrahamson, M.D., and E. W. Pezet say this about epilepsy. "Among the signs and symptoms behind which hyperinsulinism (low blood suger) masqueraded, (Doctor) Seale Harris included those of *petit mal* (mild epilepsy). It is significant, therefore, that some women who suffered from epilepsy appeared to improve during pregnancy, as rheumatoid arthritis and peptic ulcer patients did—when the blood glucose tends to be higher. Other pregnant epileptics, however, seemed to suffer more severely. A number of persons subject to epileptic seizures were given the Glucose Tolerance Test, which indicated low sugar tolerance curves. It has also been found that the brain wave tracings of persons afflicted with *petit mal* were similar to those of hyperinsulinism victims. While these facts are insufficient in themselves to indicate that epilepsy is a manifestation of hyperinsulinism, they provide enough evidence to warrant further investigation of the relationship between the two diseases."

In the *Journal of the American Medical Association* for August 15, 1966, an editorial comments on the possible treatment of epilepsy by a high fat diet—the "ketogenic diet". This is the kind of diet recommended by Dr. Robert Atkins in his book, *Dr. Atkins' Diet Revolution*. Carbohydrate is cut to the bare minimum. Patients are told to eat nothing but protein and fat.

The *Journal* states that 30 per cent of properly selected epileptic children have their seizures controlled by the high fat diet, an additional 30 per cent will show improvement in the frequency of seizures, and 40 per cent will not be influenced.

The editorial then recounts the results of an experiment reported in *Archives of Neurology*, August, 1966. Eleven children were given a diet in which about one-fourth was protein and carbohydrate, the other three-fourths fat. In five of these children epileptic attacks ceased immediately; in four the improvement in seizure control was 60 to 80 per cent; in the remaining two the high fat could not be maintained, so we do not know what the results would have been. The diets were continued for two years, "in a gradually decreasing ratio," which means, we suppose, that the amount of fat was gradually decreased and the amounts of protein and carbohydrate increased. The children remained well and either ceased having attacks or had them much less frequently. And they appeared to suffer no harm from the large amount of fat they were eating.

The Lancet for February 24, 1968 discusses schizophrenia and epilepsy as opposite sides of the same coin—that is, biologically antagonistic diseases. The author gives extensive references to earlier papers that have shown that epilepsy does not appear among people who are schizophrenic, and that, on the contrary, a considerable number of people who suffer from schizophrenia also suffer from epilepsy.

In addition, it seems that an anti-convulsant drug given to epileptics can bring on a condition of schizophrenia and, more recently, the discovery that tranquilizers given to schizophrenics can precipitate epileptic attacks.

With the characteristic tunnel-vision of the medical profession, it seems never to occur to these researchers that the same condition that causes schizophrenia might well be the same condition that causes epilepsy. Somehow, doctors seem obliged to disregard any simple explanation of illness and seek out only the most complicated and arcane explanations. Does it not seem possible that the drugs given to correct the schizophrenia caused low blood sugar which produced the epilepsy and that the drugs given to prevent epilepsy somehow so twisted and perverted the mechanism for delivering sugar to brain and nerve cells that schizophrenia resulted! Why is it impossible for doctors to see that both conditions may be simply manifestations of blood sugar disorder as are diabetes and hypoglycemia?

Why must most doctors set diabetes in one category and

deny that there is any category of disease resulting from the opposite of diabetes? Why must they decide that epilepsy is one set of conditions having nothing to do with diet and schizophrenia is another set of conditions having nothing to do with diet? Why not, in all four instances, try *first* to treat the conditions with the same sensible, highly nutritious diet and see what the results will be?

The mechanism that is disordered in all four conditions involves the immeasurably complex process by which sugar is fed to brain and nerve cells. They must have a constant supply of sugar or they will malfunction. Is it not possible that the way in which sugar is kept from brain and nerve cells in different individuals may determine whether they get epilepsy or schizophrenia, diabetes or low blood sugar? Individuals differ in their response to stress and lack of sugar in brain and nerve cells is stress.

In *Exhaustion, Causes and Treatment*, by Sam E. Roberts, M.D., a number of cases of epilepsy are described. All were successfully treated with the diet for low blood sugar. A 12-year-old girl habitually had "fainting spells" when she had been without food for long periods of time—going to mass without breakfast, for example.

From sixth grade on she had severe headaches. Away at boarding school she continued to have "fainting spells," headaches and an unsightly case of acne. Physicians tested her for brain tumor and schizophrenia. One diagnosed epilepsy. She was brought to Dr. Roberts. He gave her the lengthy Glucose Tolerance Test and the diet recommended for hypoglycemia. Within two weeks she felt so much better that she had much more energy and was delighted that she was not really schizophrenic.

One day she had a relapse because she had not gotten up early enough to eat breakfast, and had gone off to school fasting. Apparently her "fainting spells" had been epileptic attacks which occurred, as one would expect, when she had little food.

A 22-year-old patient with epilepsy came to Dr. Roberts

complaining also of headaches and exhaustion. He placed her on a diet for hypoglycemia without giving her a glucose tolerance test. She had no seizures for four months. He gave her the test, then, and discovered that it appeared to be normal. But she still had no seizures while she continued on the diet.

A 75-year-old traveling man came to the doctor with his own diagnosis. Said he, "I have had hypoglycemia and epileptic seizures for 65 years." Whenever he overworked, lost his temper or went without food too long he had a seizure. The ends of his fingers would tingle. The tingling would gradually work up to his face. His eyes would not focus, his tongue became thick and he could not talk—only mumble. Then a severe headache began. Sometimes he became delirious and fevered.

His daughter suffered from the same condition and eventually died in such an attack diagnosed as a heart attack. Later her son developed the same conditions. The original patient, put on a strict diet which excluded all sugar, remained free of attacks.

Another patient, aged 48, came to Dr. Roberts complaining of exhaustion, nervousness, tension, depression, dizziness, gas, indigestion, stomach and colon troubles. He had lost all his teeth by the age of 26. He suffered from many "blackouts". He had been told by other physicians it was all "nerves".

His diet was shocking, says Dr. Roberts. He ate mostly milk and crackers, had only two small servings of meat a week and avoided almost all other foods because they contained, he said, "too much acid". One thing wrong with him was that he *lacked* acid in his stomach, rather than having too much. In four hours during the Glucose Tolerance Test his blood sugar dropped from 80 to slightly over 40, at which point he collapsed, was put to bed and given food. Put on the hypoglycemia diet he was cooperative. He now enjoys meat, eggs, fruits, vegetables and other highly nutritious foods. Has had no blackouts or other troubles for many years.

CHAPTER 21

Can We Prevent
Peptic Ulcers?

ULCERS HAVE BECOME almost the badge of professional
honor among modern businessmen, executives, government officials and others in our Western industrialized
world. In many parts of the world, however, they are
completely unknown. Are they, in truth, the result of
today's enormous stress, or are they, as we have already
mentioned, the product of bad eating habits?

Dr. Benjamin P. Sandler has published a number of
books and papers on hypoglycemia, and, in 1940, he
published a paper in *The Review of Gastroenterology* on
how to control the pain of ulcers with a low-carbohydrate
diet. Since 1937, in fact, Dr. Sandler has performed
hundreds of tests, particularly at the Veterans Administration Hospital in Oteen, North Carolina, on patients to look
for low blood sugar tendencies. He has found, he says, low
blood sugar levels in more than half of them. "I have
concluded that any human can experience low blood sugar
as long as he or she consumes sugar and starch," Dr.
Sandler says.

Dr. T. L. Cleave, Surgeon Captain of the Royal Navy,
attributes many of our modern-day ills to what he calls "the
saccharine disease." Tooth decay is the first obvious result
of the consumption of refined cereals and sugar. Peptic

116

ulcer is another. Protein is the only food material that neutralizes the gastric acid in the stomach. It "buffers" the stomach wall against attack by the acid digestive juices. When you remove most or all of the protein from food, this buffering power is gone. Peptic ulcer is the result.

"Although many ailments involving the gastrointestinal tract are poorly understood, they are among the most common illnesses in the country, ranking second only to diseases of the heart and circulation in the number of physician office visits or house calls," states the National Institute of Arthritis and Metabolic Diseases, Public Health Service, Bethesda, Maryland.

"Peptic ulcer or peptic ulcer symptoms will strike about 10 per cent of all adults in the United States at some time in their lives," the government agency continues. "Diseases of the stomach and intestine may afflict persons of any age, but most often affect those in the middle-aged groups at the peak of their most vigorous and productive periods, often causing prolonged and expensive hospitalization and countless social and emotional problems."

Dr. T. L. Cleave tells us that in parts of Africa where white sugar and white flour products are unknown, peptic ulcer is also practically unknown. In one hospital, only two cases turned up in 25,000 hospital admissions.

"The gastric juice manufactured by the stomach contains hydrochloric acid, mucus and a ferment, pepsin, which breaks down protein in the food into simpler substances," reports *The Book of Health*. "Sometimes the mechanism for secreting gastric acids does not shut off after all the food has been consumed, and the pepsin-hydrochloric acid mixture goes to work on the digestive tract itself. Thus, a peptic ulcer occurs in the walls of the stomach or the duodenum which are the regions bathed by the gastric juices. Peptic ulcers may also occur in the esophagus as a result of the backflow of juices.

"The vagus nerve is believed to be largely responsible for the continuous overproduction of gastric acids... It is sometimes overactive at night when there is no food in the stomach. The juices go directly through the pylorus into the duodenum (the first portion of the small intestine). This causes destruction of the mucous membrane of the intestine and can result in a duodenal ulcer . . . People with a low concentration of hydrochloric acid in their gastric juices rarely develop peptic ulcer," *The Book of Health* states.

One school of thought in medical literature is that peptic ulcer is psychological, the result of stress. Two Washington physicians were quoted in *The New York Times* as saying that surgery for ulcers accomplishes nothing. The patient just develops a new set of symptoms, because he wants to have something to complain about, they said.

In elaborate and expensive experiments laboratory scientists have uncovered, they think, evidence that frustration and anxiety do cause stomach ulcers. Most orthodox medical literature, however, does not ever suggest that the same food habits which caused the ulcer may be causing the other symptoms, or even causing the frustration and anxiety.

There is considerable evidence that drugs of various kinds may play a role. Coffee and nicotine, as well as a number of medical drugs—especially aspirin—appear to be able to start the process which culminates in a full-blown ulcer.

Since ulcers are treated chiefly by diet, and all food and drink we take in goes directly to the stomach, one would think that thoughtful researchers would study first the effects of diet in causing ulcers. But such thinking is rare, possibly because we have been brain-washed into believing that everything is so wholesome at the supermarket that it could not possibly be responsible for such a devastating disorder as ulcer, which afflicts such a large number of Americans.

A Danish physician suggested in *Nordisk Medicine*, February 27, 1964, that lack of protein in the diet can cause ulcer. He said that during war years, when there was less meat available in Norway, ulcer incidence increased.

Before and after the war, when plenty of meat protein was available, incidence of ulcers decreased. But it is well to remember that the part we remove from foods when they are refined and processed is the high protein part. So, in essence, we are removing the protein from flour and sugarcane when we make them into refined cereal and flour and pure white sugar. Could this be related to present-day ulcer incidence?

Dr. T. L. Cleave thinks that it could. And in his book, *Peptic Ulcer*, he presents his arguments which seem to be eminently sound. He says that the protein of foods is, indeed, the "buffer" that protects our stomachs from ulcers. When we remove it from foods and put into our stomachs foods which have been "stripped" of their protein by refining, we practically guarantee ulcers as a result.

Stress a cause of ulcers? Nonsense, says Dr. Cleave. "If there is one thing that every single organism on this planet knows and is equipped to deal with, after a remorseless struggle extending over several thousand million years, it is stress in all its shapes and forms.. The time may be approaching," he goes on, when... the facile explanation that peptic ulcer is a disease due to mental stress may seem as remote from the truth as the view that malaria is caused by vapors rising from the swamps.

"... The incidence of peptic ulcer in every country rises or falls with the high or low consumption of carbohydrate foods that have suffered removal of protein, by refining," says Dr. Cleave.

The refining of food makes it possible for us to eat more of it than we would if it were in its natural state, Dr. Cleave reminds us. The average individual in England—and in the U.S. as well—eats five ounces of refined sugar a day. Five ounces of refined sugar are made from two and a half pounds of sugar cane or beets. Obviously, none of us would carry along a snack to the movies consisting of over two pounds of a bulky, fibrous food like sugar cane. Nor could we contemplate eating such a quantity of heavy, tough, chewy food over a whole day. But we can very easily eat five ounces of sugar in candy or soft drinks, on an empty stomach, with not a particle of protein present in our stomachs to buffer the disastrous effects of this amount of refined sugar on the stomach lining. We already know what this might do to blood sugar levels.

At coffee break and perhaps several other times during the day we may pour coffee or tea, heavily laden with sugar, into an empty stomach. And the coffee is often accompanied by a sticky sweet, such as a donut. It is extremely important, says Dr. Cleave, that we have enough protein with every meal and that the protein be distributed evenly throughout the meal. This is one reason why sugary desserts may cause damage even though you eat them at meal times. The protein part of the meal may already be almost through your stomach by the time your dessert arrives there.

Ulcer patients may be suffering from a serious lack of vitamin C, according to a series of letters in the *British Medical Journal*. One Glasgow physician investigated the state of 109 ulcer patients in regard to their vitamin C condition. He found that patients with ulcers showed "evidence of depletion of vitamin C" as well as patients who had other complications along with ulcer.

Some patients who had had ulcer surgery and were in good health were found to have normal levels of the vitamin, but others showed depletion "despite an apparently normal dietary intake." Dr. Iain W. Dymock concludes that patients with duodenal ulcers are short on vitamin C. He believes the reason may have to do with absorption. In addition, he says that antacid drugs given by many physicians may have an effect on absorption. He says that all of his patients have responded well to vitamin C supplements.

Medical World News, commenting on the work of two other Scots physicians, says that ulcer patients generally seem to get less vitamin C in their food. And, after they have had surgery for their ulcers, the level of vitamin C in their bodies does not return to normal, even though they begin to eat plenty of vitamin C-rich food.

They quote Dr. Max M. Cohen as saying that, in times of stress, there is increased use of vitamin C by the body tissues, especially wounded tissues. In surgical patients, too little vitamin C may mean that a wound will not heal properly, or may even open again, after an apparent healing.

The Glasgow doctors believe that the low blood levels of vitamin C in ulcer patients are due to just plain not getting enough of the vitamin in food. But they also speculate on how large a part lack of absorption may play, since the digestive tract must contain plenty of hydrochloric acid in order to assimilate vitamin C. Ulcer patients are given drugs to shut off the flow of hydrochloric acid in their stomachs.

If you want to avoid peptic ulcers—which occur about four times more frequently in men than in women—avoid the foods and food habits that cause ulcer. Perhaps worst of all is the eating of pure sugar on an empty stomach. Candy and soft drinks are two of the worst offenders.

Drinking coffee or liquor and smoking cigarettes are other habits that stimulate the stomach to produce the acid which destroys the stomach lining, unless there is a "buffer" present. If you must drink a little coffee, drink it with a meal, never before, between or after the meal. The same applies to alcoholic beverages, tea and soft drinks.

Finally, don't smoke!

CHAPTER 22

Nobody Should Have Gout These Days

GOUT, THE MYSTERIOUS, excruciatingly painful disorder which has a long history of afflicting mostly the rich, the highly intelligent and the prominent, has now become commonplace among the rest of us mortals. More and more people are coming to .their doctors these days complaining of the sudden, intense pain, usually in a toe, which is a symptom of gout.

It was well known in early Greek and Roman days and throughout Europe during more recent centuries. Benjamin Franklin and Frederick the Great were victims of gout. Painful, crippling and deforming, this disorder comes and goes in the people it afflicts, seeming to come on almost overnight under stress of some emotional strain.

There seems to be little doubt that the tendency to have gout is inherited. Most recent research seems to show that, if you are a person with gout, you may have inherited a larger than normal requirement for some nutrient. If, throughout your life, you supply this nutrient in ample quantity—that means much more than the average person needs—you can probably avoid attacks of gout.

"Gout is a metabolic disease in which high levels of uric acid in the blood are characteristic," states *The Book of Health*, 3rd edition. "It is not known whether these levels

122

result from an excessive production of uric acid or from its inadequate excretion by the kidneys, or from both factors.

"The onset of the first acute attack of gout is marked by sudden and excruciating pain in a joint," *The Book of Health* continues. "Within hours, the affected joint is hot, red, swollen and extremely tender. In 70 per cent of the cases, the large toe is affected by the initial attack. In subsequent attacks, an increasing number of joints are involved, especially those of the knees, ankles, feet, hip, shoulders, elbows, wrists and hands. The disease more commonly attacks joints of the lower extremities."

The uric acid, in crystal form, gathers around joints and tissues and causes painful inflammation. Formerly, it was thought that this overabundance of uric acid was the result of eating lots of meat and other foods containing "purines." Today, it is generally recognized that the body makes excessive uric acid itself, regardless of how much there is in the food eaten.

Research in Geneva, Switzerland in 1968 seemed to show a correlation between gout and diabetes and other abnormalities of blood sugar regulation. High blood pressure and very high blood levels of fatty substances showed up in a group of volunteers with primary gout. "Gout clearly preceded diabetes," says E. Martin of Policlinique Universitaire de Medicin in Geneva.

Dr. John Yudkin, in his excellent book, *Sweet and Dangerous*, is more specific in suggesting that sugar—that demon of blood sugar regulation—may be a contributing factor to gout. He says that gout occurs mostly in middle age and older, and more in men than in women.

"One of the features often found in people with atherosclerosis, and found in almost all people with gout, is a raised level of uric acid in the blood . . . Some Italian research workers have shown that the ingestion of fructose . . . causes an increase in the level of uric acid in the blood . . . There is some indication that people with gout are rather more likely to get atherosclerosis than are other people, and, conversely, that people with atherosclerosis are more likely to have gout," Dr. Yudkin reports.

While studying patients with gout, Dr. Yudkin and his colleagues also studied those with rheumatoid arthritis. The patients with rheumatoid arthritis were eating about the same amount of sugar as the controls, but "the patients with gout were taking appreciably more sugar than the control subjects; the median values were 102 grams of sugar a day for the gouty patients and 54 grams for the control subjects."

Another indication that gout may be due to nutritional indiscretions was revealed in a survey of 922 employees of a large industrial firm who were known or suspected to be problem drinkers. The results showed that these people had a higher incidence of gout, high blood pressure, cirrhosis of the liver, stomach ulcer, asthma, diabetes, neuritis, cerebrovascular disease (which leads to strokes) and heart disease. We have already documented how most of these disorders can be directly related to a pattern of inadequate nutrition, with overemphasis on refined carbohydrates.

In *Let's Get Well*, Adelle Davis tells us that pantothenic acid, one of the B vitamins discovered by Dr. Roger J. Williams of the University of Texas, is responsible for turning uric acid into harmless substances that are easily excreted. If there is not enough pantothenic acid in the diet to process all the uric acid being manufactured, it will collect and cause trouble.

"Gout is an arthritis-like disease which is characterized by deposits of uric acid salts in and near the joints. This, among other things, impairs lubrication," writes Dr. Roger J. Williams in his informative book, *Nutrition Against Disease*. "Gout has long been thought of as resulting from 'high living,' particularly intemperate eating. Biochemical individuality enters here also, and makes some individuals peculiarly susceptible."

Dr. Williams reports that, in a study of 11 healthy young men, one of them, after repeated tests, showed uric acid levels in his blood 26 per cent higher than the other 10 men, and 50 per cent higher than one of the volunteers. "The mere presence of high uric acid in the blood is not enough to cause gout; its salts must be precipitated in and around the joints, and this does not always happen in individuals who have a high content of uric acid in the blood," Dr. Williams says.

"One of the time-honored measures to be taken in the case of gout is to avoid consuming food that contains substantial amounts of nucleic acids (sweetbreads, for example), because nucleic acids give rise to uric acid in the body," Dr. Williams continues. "Nucleic acids and uric acid, like cholesterol, are produced in the body, however, and their avoidance in food may not effectively prevent uric acid piling up in the blood or its salts from being precipitated to settle in the joints ... Gout is closely related to arthritis, and in some cases arthritic deposits are suggestive of gout."

A lack of vitamin E can also cause trouble. Animals lacking in this important vitamin excrete far more uric acid than normal animals on a normal diet. And when the deficient animals are given enough vitamin E, the overproduction of uric acid stops.

Adelle Davis explains that, in the early days before refrigeration, rich people ate mostly meat, since bread and vegetables were considered to be food for the poor. Without refrigeration, much of the meat was spoiled and its fat was rancid. Rancid fat destroys vitamin E almost instantaneously, so gout—"the rich man's disease"—caused by vitamin E deficiency may have been common in those days. The poorer people who lived mostly on freshly baked black bread, rich in vitamin E and the B vitamins, did not suffer from gout.

Today, we have a wide variety of foods available for all, and refrigeration is universal. But rancid fats still pose a problem in such things as salted nuts and popcorn, which may be quite stale in the packages in which you buy them, stale chopped nuts, and, particularly cooking fats that are used again and again for French fries and other horrors.

LOW BLOOD SUGAR

The relationship between alcohol and gout has been studied extensively. An Australian study in 1967 showed a correlation between alcohol consumption, especially beer, and uric acid levels of blood. Cigarette smoking also appeared to be part of the picture. Alcohol and smoking both have a decided effect on blood sugar levels, so this is not surprising.

Some doctors may still be prescribing for gout patients the old diets which forbade foods containing purines. These include many of our best foods: liver, kidney, heart, anchovies, sardines, meat extracts. Foods only a little less rich in purines are: meat, fowl, fish, lentils, whole grain cereals, yeast, legumes, mushrooms. Some diets for gout patients allow one serving of such foods per day. High protein foods that do not contain much purine are: milk, cheese and eggs. Fruits and vegetables are relatively free of this substance, which is a white crystalline compound which is the parent substance of a group of compounds, including uric acid, caffeine and xanthine.

In the early days of her career, when she was a nutrition consultant to many physicians, Adelle Davis reports on one woman whose husband had gout. The woman said that she had given her husband large amounts of liver and brewers yeast. Miss Davis, alarmed, said that this was the wrong thing to do because both foods are so high in purine. "But my husband is better than he's ever been before," the woman exclaimed.

If your doctor tells you to avoid purines in food, avoid those mentioned above, but do make sure you are getting plenty of protein by eating enough milk, cheese and eggs. Get plenty of vitamin E, either in foods or supplements. Also make sure that you are getting ample pantothenic acid. And lay off the sweets, especially sugar.

Avoid rancid fats like the plague. Do not eat fatty foods unless you know where they came from and how long they have been prepared. Shun all prepared "convenience" foods—TV dinners, frozen fried foods, salted nuts, potato chips, French fries, etc. Do not re-use fats for cooking.

Throw out the bacon fat and the chicken fat after it has been heated once. Don't re-heat and use again. Finally, learn to read labels diligently. You'll be surprised at what you will find in many of your favorite foods.

CHAPTER 23

Suggested Menus for the Hypoglycemic

HOW DO YOU go about planning a diet like the one recommended in this book? The individual foods don't matter much, so long as you observe carefully what *kind* of foods they are (protein, carbohydrate, fat) and how often you must eat. The way you prepare foods is also not important, so long as you limit foods which contain lots of carbohydrate—that is, starch and sugar. Use your time-tested recipes. You may eat whatever vegetables you prefer, but go easy on the very starchy ones like lima beans, potatoes, navy beans and so on. We have suggested low-carbohydrate ones instead. It is also advisable to eat plenty of dark, green leafy vegetables like broccoli, spinach and salad greens because of their fiber content and their vitamins and minerals.

Only if you are accustomed to serving pre-packaged "convenience" foods from the supermarket will you have to make real changes in your menus and ways of doing things. "Convenience" foods are those you should be most careful to avoid, along with all bakery products, and confectionery, soft drinks and any other source of sugar.

Fruit juices must be unsweetened. Do not drink prune or grape juice. Too sweet. If you have a weight problem, tomato juice is best, since it is lowest in carbohydrate. You may have any fruit except the dried ones like dates, figs and prunes. You may have cream in any beverage, but no sugar of any kind. No honey, no molasses, no corn syrup. Gelatin must be the plain, unflavored kind. Avoid especially high carbohydrate foods: pasta, noodles, macaroni, pancakes, waffles. Bread should be as high in protein as possible. Make your own from real whole grain flour, if possible, well enriched with high protein supplements like yeast, wheat germ and bran. These are available at your health food store.

If you don't like some of the foods listed here, then don't eat them, *but don't substitute something starchy or sugary.* If you dislike seafood, substitute beef, pork or chicken. If you don't like asparagus, substitute green beans, squash or some vegetable you do like. There is nothing magical about the arrangement or variety of foods listed here. We are only trying to encourage you to eat foods high in protein and to avoid foods high in any kind of carbohydrates, and to avoid completely *all* refined carbohydrates.

We have made up these menus from plain, well-known, popular American dishes familiar to most of us. We have not included recipes. If you want to go to a lot of fuss and prepare "gourmet" foods instead, that's fine. Use any recipe you have, but omit anything starchy or sweet. If your sauerbraten recipe calls for sugar or ginger snaps, don't use them. If you make spaghetti and meat balls, eat the meat balls but not the spaghetti. If you'd rather have Beef Strogonoff than pot roast, fine. Make it with all the sour cream and yogurt the recipe calls for. But don't serve it on noodles or rice. Have a low carbohydrate vegetable instead.

When you eat in a restaurant, observe the same rules. Order plain meat, fish, seafood or poultry dishes which you know will contain no starchy or sugary ingredients. Eat low carbohydrate vegetables and lots of salad. Do not order dessert unless there is fresh fruit on the menu. Ask for Sanka rather than coffee. Most restaurants serve it these days.

Let's plan menus for two weeks. Any of these menus may be substituted for any others. You may eat approximately the same thing day after day if you choose to. You may switch dinner to the early morning hours and eat your breakfast at night, if you prefer. You may have a different menu every single day and eat up every leftover at the next meal if you wish. You may eat lunch at night and have your larger meal at noontime, if you prefer.

The only thing you *must* remember is to watch very carefully the amount of high carbohydrate food you eat. And you must eat something at regular intervals during the day—those intervals which we spell out in these pages. After several months, when your symptoms have disappeared, you may relax some of the rules. Have only one snack, if you want it, after dinner. Have a baked potato or some lima beans or corn from time to time. But do not relax the rules for eating three meals a day (especially breakfast). Have a high protein snack if you get hungry between meals.

And swear off sweets for the rest of your life. You'll find you don't want them. You will lose your craving for sweets if you faithfully follow these recommendations. Your between-meal hunger pangs will disappear. You will eat less and enjoy it more. We promise you. And you will eat more economically, for all those sugary goodies which don't really nourish you are expensive. Pound for pound, the essential nutrients they contain are far more expensive than the nutrients in foods like meat, fish, poultry, egg, and dairy products, although prices on these foods may appear to be higher. It's the nutrients that count. And sugar-rich foods are the most expensive ones there are, in terms of good nutrition and good health.

Menus

Monday

On arising—a medium orange, half grapefruit or ½ cup (4 oz.) juice, preferably tomato juice.

Breakfast: Mushroom omelet; bacon; only one slice of bread or toast, well buttered, decaffeinated coffee, weak tea, herb tea, milk or buttermilk.

Two hours after breakfast—½ cup (4 oz.) juice.

Lunch: Cold cuts (any you prefer, in any quantity), only one slice of bread, well buttered, watercress salad, decaffeinated coffee, weak tea, herb tea, milk or buttermilk.

Three hours after lunch: 1 cup of milk, buttermilk or yogurt or a large chunk of cheese.

One hour before dinner: ½ glass of juice, preferably tomato juice.

Dinner: Liberal portion of meat loaf; buttered spinach; baked zucchini; tossed salad with lots of dressing; half grapefruit; decaffeinated coffee, weak tea, herb tea, milk or buttermilk.

Two-three hours after dinner—1 cup milk.

Every two hours until bedtime—½ cup milk or small handful of nuts.

Tuesday

On arising—a medium orange, half grapefruit or ½ cup (4 oz.) juice, preferably tomato juice.

Breakfast: Poached eggs; only one slice of bread or toast, well buttered; cottage cheese, decaffeinated coffee, weak tea, herb tea, buttermilk or milk.

Two hours after breakfast: ½ cup (4 oz.) juice.

Lunch: Cheeseburger with bacon; only one slice of bread; coleslaw with carrots; half an orange; decaffeinated coffee, weak tea, herb tea, milk or buttermilk.

Three hours after lunch: one cup of milk, buttermilk or yogurt, or a large chunk of cheese.

One hour before dinner: one-half cup of juice.

Dinner: Roast chicken; buttered Brussels sprouts; boiled onions; avocado salad; watermelon; decaffeinated coffee, weak tea, herb tea, milk or buttermilk.

Two-three hours after dinner—1 cup milk.

Every two hours until bedtime—½ cup milk or small handful of nuts.

Wednesday

On arising—one medium orange, half grapefruit or ½ cup (4 oz.) juice, preferably tomato juice.

Breakfast: Sausage and fried eggs; yogurt or cottage cheese; only one slice of bread well buttered; decaffeinated coffee, weak tea, herb tea, milk or buttermilk.

Two hours after breakfast—½ cup (4 oz.) juice.

Lunch: Open-faced chicken sandwich; only one slice of bread, as much chicken as you wish with plenty of mayonnaise or dressing; celery and radishes; half an apple; decaffeinated coffee, weak tea, herb tea, milk or buttermilk.

Three hours after lunch: 1 cup milk, buttermilk or yogurt or a large chunk of cheese.

One hour before dinner: one-half cup of juice.

Dinner: Pot roast with celery, mushrooms, peppers or cauliflower substituted for potatoes and carrots; large tossed salad with plenty of dressing; fresh pineapple, decaffeinated coffee, weak tea, herb tea, milk or buttermilk.

Two-three hours after dinner—1 cup milk.

Every two hours until bedtime—½ cup milk or small handful of nuts.

MENUS

Thursday

On arising—a medium orange, half grapefruit or ½ cup (4 oz.) juice, preferably tomato juice.

Breakfast: Ham and eggs; yogurt or cottage cheese; only one slice of bread or toast well buttered; decaffeinated coffee, weak tea, herb tea, milk or buttermilk.

Two hours after breakfast: four ounces (½ cup) juice.

Lunch: Cold roast beef; only one slice of bread or toast well buttered, olives and celery; fresh apple and cheese; decaffeinated coffee, weak tea, herb tea, milk or buttermilk.

Three hours after lunch: 1 cup milk, buttermilk or yogurt or one large chunk of cheese.

One hour before dinner: one-half cup of juice.

Dinner: Ground lamb patties; snow peas, buttered cauliflower; radishes and celery; half grapefruit; decaffeinated coffee, weak tea, herb tea, milk or buttermilk.

Two-three hours after dinner—1 cup milk.

Every two hours until bedtime—½ cup milk or small handful nuts.

Friday

On arising: one medium orange, half grapefruit or ½ cup (4 oz.) juice, preferably tomato juice.

Breakfast: Scrambled eggs and bacon; cottage cheese, only one slice of bread well buttered; decaffeinated coffee, weak tea, herb tea, milk or buttermilk.

Two hours after breakfast: ½ cup (4 oz.) juice.

Lunch: Sauteed chicken livers or liverwurst sandwich; only one slice of bread, well buttered; tomato and onion salad; one fresh apricot; decaffeinated coffee, weak tea, herb tea, milk or buttermilk.

Three hours after lunch: 1 cup milk, buttermilk, yogurt or one large chunk of cheese.

One hour before dinner: one-half cup of juice.

Dinner: Broiled or fried fish of any kind; summer squash; buttered green beans with almonds; Waldorf salad; decaffeinated coffee, weak tea, herb tea, milk or buttermilk.

Two-three hours after dinner—1 cup milk.

Every two hours until bedtime—½ cup milk or small handful of nuts.

Saturday

On arising: one orange, one-half grapefruit or ½ cup (4 oz.) juice, preferably tomato juice.

Breakfast: Creamed chipped beef; only one slice of toast, well buttered; yogurt or cottage cheese; decaffeinated coffee, weak tea, herb tea, milk or buttermilk.

Two hours after breakfast: ½ cup (4 oz.) juice.

Lunch: Clam chowder; peanut or almond butter sandwich on only one slice of bread; hard-cooked egg; apple and nuts; decaffeinated coffee, weak tea, herb tea, milk or buttermilk.

Three hours after lunch: 1 cup milk, buttermilk, yogurt or one large chunk of cheese.

One hour before dinner: one-half cup (4 oz.) juice.

Dinner: Crab or shrimp meat in brown butter; asparagus; buttered beets; tomatoes and scallions; fresh pear, decaffeinated coffee, weak tea, herb tea, milk or buttermilk.

Two-three hours after dinner—1 cup milk.

Every two hours until bedtime—½ cup milk or small handful of nuts.

Sunday

On arising: one orange, one-half grapefruit or ½ cup (4 oz.) juice, preferably tomato juice.

Breakfast: Poached eggs; bacon; only one slice of bread or toast, well buttered; decaffeinated coffee, weak tea, herb tea, milk or buttermilk.

Two hours after breakfast: ½ cup (4 oz.) juice.

Lunch: Grilled cheese sandwich (lots of cheese and only one slice of bread); peanut butter on wholegrain crackers; carrot sticks and cucumbers; half cantaloupe; decaffeinated coffee, weak tea, herb tea, milk or buttermilk.

Three hours after lunch: 1 cup milk, buttermilk or yogurt or one big chunk of cheese.

One hour before dinner: one-half cup (4 oz.) juice.

Dinner: Corned beef and cabbage; lettuce, tomato and onion salad; fresh apple and nuts; decaffeinated coffee, weak tea, herb tea, milk or buttermilk.

Two-three hours after dinner—1 cup milk.

Every two hours until bedtime—½ cup milk or small handful of nuts.

SECOND WEEK

Monday

On arising: one orange, half-grapefruit or ½ cup (4 oz.) juice, preferably tomato.

Breakfast: Canadian bacon; scrambled eggs; only one slice of bread or toast, well buttered; decaffeinated coffee, weak tea, herb tea, milk or buttermilk.

Two hours after breakfast: ½ cup (4 oz.) milk or juice.

Lunch: Salmon salad; only one slice of bread, well buttered; cucumbers in yogurt; decaffeinated coffee, weak tea, herb tea, milk or buttermilk.

Three hours after lunch: 1 cup milk, buttermilk, yogurt, or one large chunk of cheese.

One hour before dinner: one-half cup (4 oz.) juice.

Dinner: Barbecued chicken; fried eggplant; buttered cauliflower; tomato aspic with lots of salad greens and dressing; tangerine; decaffeinated coffee, weak tea, herb tea, milk or buttermilk.

Two-three hours after dinner—1 cup milk.

Every two hours until bedtime—½ cup milk or small handful of nuts.

Tuesday

On arising: one orange, half-grapefruit or ½ cup (4 oz.) juice, preferably tomato juice.

Breakfast: Hamburger; only one piece of toast or bread, well buttered; cottage cheese or yogurt; decaffeinated coffee, weak tea, herb tea, milk or buttermilk.

Two hours after breakfast: ½ cup (4 oz.) juice.

Lunch: Chicken salad; only one slice of bread, well buttered; whole tomato sliced with mayonnaise; watermelon; decaffeinated coffee, weak tea, herb tea, milk or buttermilk

Three hours after lunch: 1 cup milk, buttermilk, yogurt or one large chunk of cheese.

One hour before dinner: one-half cup (4 oz.) juice.

Dinner: Broiled or fried liver with bacon or onions or both; stewed tomatoes; buttered broccoli; cottage cheese and pear salad; decaffeinated coffee, weak tea, herb tea, milk or buttermilk.

Two-three hours after dinner—1 cup milk.

Every two hours until bedtime—½ cup milk or small handful of nuts.

Wednesday

On arising: one orange, half-grapefruit or ½ cup (4 oz.) juice.

Breakfast: Scrambled eggs with cheese; ham; only one slice of bread or toast well buttered; decaffeinated coffee, weak tea, herb tea, milk or buttermilk.

Two hours after breakfast: ½ cup (4 oz.) milk or juice.

Lunch: Cheeseburger with bacon; only one slice of bread well buttered; carrot curls, olives and celery; apple and nuts; decaffeinated coffee, weak tea, herb tea, milk or buttermilk.

Three hours after lunch: 1 cup milk, buttermilk, yogurt or one large chunk of cheese.

One hour before dinner: one-half cup (4 oz.) juice.

Dinner: Pork and sauerkraut; one small dip of mashed potatoes; cucumber salad; blueberries in yogurt; decaffeinated coffee, weak tea, herb tea, milk or buttermilk.

Two hours after dinner—1 cup milk.

Every two hours until bedtime—½ cup milk or small handful of nuts.

Thursday

On arising: one orange, half-grapefruit or ½ cup (4 oz.) juice.

Breakfast: Soft boiled eggs with crisp bacon crumbled into them; only one slice of bread or toast well buttered; cheese; decaffeinated coffee, weak tea, herb tea, milk or buttermilk.

Two hours after breakfast: one half cup (4 oz.) milk or juice.

Lunch: Green peppers stuffed with tuna salad; only one slice of bread well buttered; half grapefruit; decaffeinated coffee, weak tea, herb tea, milk or buttermilk.

Three hours after lunch: 1 cup milk, buttermilk or yogurt, or one large chunk of cheese.

One hour before dinner: one-half cup (4 oz.) juice.

Dinner: London broil; buttered turnips; creamed peas; tossed salad; banana; decaffeinated coffee, weak tea, herb tea, milk or buttermilk.

Two-three hours after dinner—1 cup milk.

Every two hours until bedtime—½ cup milk or small handful nuts.

Friday

Upon arising: one orange, half grapefruit or ½ cup (4 oz.) juice, preferably tomato juice.

Breakfast: Baked eggs; broiled fish fillet; only one slice of bread well buttered; decaffeinated coffee, weak tea, herb tea, milk or buttermilk.

Two hours after breakfast: four ounces (½ cup) milk or juice.

Lunch: Crab salad; cream cheese and pimiento on one slice of bread; celery and radishes; decaffeinated coffee, weak tea, milk or buttermilk.

Three hours after lunch: 1 cup milk, buttermilk or yogurt or one large chunk of cheese.

One hour before dinner: one-half cup juice.

Dinner: Roast lamb; green beans; buttered carrots; tossed salad; cheese and nuts; decaffeinated coffee, weak tea, herb tea, milk or buttermilk.

Two-three hours after dinner—1 cup milk.

Every two hours until bedtime—½ cup milk or small handful nuts.

MENUS

Saturday

On arising: one medium orange, half grapefruit or ½ cup (4 oz.) juice, preferably tomato juice.

Breakfast: Smoked fish; one poached egg; only one slice of bread or toast, well buttered; decaffeinated coffee, weak tea, herb tea, milk or buttermilk.

Two hours after breakfast: one-half cup (4 oz.) juice.

Lunch: Chef's salad with plenty of cold meat, chicken and/or cheese; only one slice of bread, well buttered; decaffeinated coffee, weak tea, herb tea, milk or buttermilk.

Three hours after lunch: 1 cup milk, buttermilk, yogurt or one large chunk of cheese.

One hour before dinner: one-half cup (4 oz.) juice.

Dinner: Baked ham; buttered beets; cauliflower; raw vegetable-gelatin salad; apple and nuts; decaffeinated coffee, weak tea, herb tea; milk or buttermilk.

Two-three hours after dinner—1 cup milk.

Every two hours until bedtime—½ cup milk or small handful nuts.

Sunday

On arising: one medium orange, half grapefruit or ½ cup (4 oz.) juice, preferably tomato juice.

Breakfast: Canadian bacon; fried eggs; only one slice of bread or toast, well buttered; decaffeinated coffee, weak tea, herb tea, milk or buttermilk.

Two hours after breakfast: one-half cup (4 oz.) juice.

Lunch: Ham salad; tomatoes and cucumbers; one fresh apricot; decaffeinated coffee, weak tea, herb tea, milk or buttermilk.

Three hours after lunch: 1 cup milk, buttermilk or yogurt or one large chunk of cheese.

One hour before dinner: one-half cup (4 oz.) juice.

Dinner: Broiled steak; creamed spinach, acorn squash; tossed salad; nuts and cheese; decaffeinated coffee, weak tea, herb tea; milk or buttermilk.

Two-three hours after dinner—1 cup milk.

Every two hours until bedtime—½ cup milk or small handful nuts.

Bibliography

Abrahamson, E.M. and A.W. Pezet, *Body, Mind and Sugar*, Pyramid paperback, New York City, 1971.

Blaine, Judge Tom R., *Mental Health Through Nutrition*, The Citadel Press, 120 Enterprise Ave., Secaucus, N.J., 1969.

Blaine, Judge Tom R., *Goodbye, Allergies*, The Citadel Press, 120 Enterprise Ave., Secaucus, N.J., 1964.

Cheraskin, E., W.M. Ringsdorf, Jr., with Arline Brecher, *Psychodietetics*, Stein and Day, New York City, 1974.

Clark, Randolph Lee and Russel W. Cumley, *The Book of Health*, Van Nostrand and Reinhold Books, New York City, 1973.

Cleave, T.L., *The Saccharine Disease*, John Wright and Sons, Bristol, England, 1974.

Davis, Adelle, *Let's Get Well*, Harcourt Brace and World, New York City, 1965.

Roberts, Sam E., *Exhaustion, Causes and Treatment*, Rodale Book Division, Rodale Press, Emmaus, Pa., 1967.

Rosenberg, Harold, *The Doctor's Book of Vitamin Therapy*, G.P. Putnam's Sons, New York City, 1974.

Sandler, Benjamin P., *How to Prevent Heart Attacks*, Lee Foundation for Nutritional Research, Milwaukee, Wis., 1958.

Steincrohn, Peter J., *Low Blood Sugar*, Henry Regnery Co., Chicago, 1972.

Williams, Roger J., *Nutrition Against Disease*, Pitman Publishing Corp., New York City, 1971.

Yudkin, John, *Sweet and Dangerous*, Peter H. Wyden, New York City, 1972.

Explanation of
the Tables

THE VALUES SHOWN in the following tables, which are taken from *Food, The Yearbook of Agriculture*, 1959, are in terms of common units of measure, as one cup, one ounce, or a piece of specified size. The quantities of foods thus shown can be converted readily to particular serving portions. The one-cup amount, for example, can be reduced or multiplied in estimating servings of various sizes.

The cup measure used refers to the standard 8-ounce measuring cup of 8 fluid ounces or one-half liquid pint. The ounce shown is by weight, that is, one-sixteenth of a pound avoirdupois, unless the fluid ounce is indicated.

Most of the foods listed in the table are in ready-to-serve form, but a few items frequently used as ingredients in prepared dishes have been included.

Values for many of the food mixtures have been calculated from typical recipes. The cooked vegetables have no added fat.

A column showing water content is in the table, as the percentage of moisture is frequently useful in identifying and comparing food items.

Parts of some foods, as seeds, skins, bone, are either inedible or may be eaten but usually are discarded. The nutrient values in the table apply to the parts customarily eaten. Values for potato, for example, apply to potato without the skin. If the skin also is eaten, the amounts of some nutrients will be a little larger than shown in the table.

Adams and Murray are, of course, not recommending all of these foods for anyone on the hypoglycemic diet. They are printed for informational purposes only.

Nutrients in Common Foods in Terms of Household Measures

Item number	Food	Water	Food energy	Protein	Fat	Total carbohydrate	Calcium	Iron	Vitamin A value	Thiamine	Riboflavin	Niacin	Ascorbic acid
		Percent	Calories	Grams	Grams	Grams	Milligrams	Milligrams	International Units	Milligrams	Milligrams	Milligrams	Milligrams
	MILK AND MILK PRODUCTS												
	Milk; 1 cup:												
1	Fluid, whole	87	165	9	10	12	285	0.1	390	0.08	0.42	0.2	2
2	Fluid, nonfat (skim)	90	90	9	Trace	13	298	.1	10	.10	.44	.2	2
3	Buttermilk, cultured (from skim milk)	90	90	9	Trace	13	298	.1	10	.10	.44	.2	2
4	Evaporated (undiluted)	74	345	18	20	24	635	.3	820	.10	.84	.5	3
5	Condensed, sweetened (undiluted)	26	985	25	25	170	825	.3	1,020	.24	1.21	.5	3
6	Dry, whole	2	515	27	28	39	968	.5	1,160	.30	1.50	.7	6
7	Dry, nonfat	3	290	29	1	42	1,040	.5	20	.38	1.44	.7	6
8	Half and half (milk and cream)	80	330	8	29	11	259	.1	1,190	.07	.39	.2	2
	Cream; 1 tablespoon:												
9	Light, table or coffee	72	30	Trace	3	1	15	Trace	120	Trace	.02	Trace	Trace
10	Heavy or whipping	59	50	Trace	5	Trace	12	Trace	220	Trace	.02	Trace	Trace
	Milk beverages; 1 cup:												
11	Cocoa (all milk)	79	235	8	11	26	286	.9	390	.09	.45	.4	2
12	Chocolate flavored drink	83	190	8	6	27	270	.5	210	.09	.41	.2	2
13	Malted milk	78	280	12	12	32	364	.8	680	.18	.56	....	3
14	Yoghurt (from partially skimmed milk); 1 cup	89	120	8	4	13	295	.1	170	.09	.43	.2	2
	Cheese; 1 ounce:												
15	Cheddar, or American	36	115	7	9	1	221	.3	380	.01	.15	Trace	0
16	Cheddar, processed	39	105	7	9	Trace	214	.3	350	Trace	.12	Trace	0
17	Cheese foods, Cheddar	43	95	6	7	2	163	.2	300	.01	.17	Trace	0
	Cottage:												
18	From skim milk	79	25	5	Trace	1	26	.1	Trace	.01	.08	Trace	0
19	Creamed	78	30	4	1	1	25	.1	50	.01	.08	Trace	0
20	Cream cheese	51	105	2	11	1	18	.1	440	Trace	.07	Trace	0
21	Roquefort, or blue	40	105	6	9	Trace	122	.2	350	.01	.17	.1	0
22	Swiss	39	105	7	8	1	271	.3	320	.01	.06	Trace	0
	Desserts (largely milk):												
23	Cornstarch pudding, plain; 1 cup	76	275	9	10	39	290	.1	390	.07	.40	.1	2
24	Custard, baked; 1 cup, 8 fluid ounces	77	285	13	14	28	278	1.0	870	.10	.47	.2	1

143

Item number	Food	Water	Food energy	Protein	Fat	Total carbohydrate	Calcium	Iron	Vitamin A value	Thiamine	Riboflavin	Niacin	Ascorbic acid
	Ice cream, plain, factory packed:												
25	1 slice or individual brick, ⅓ quart....	62	165	3	10	17	100	.1	420	.03	.15	.1	1
26	1 container, 3½ fluid ounces....	62	130	2	8	13	76	.1	320	.03	.12	.1	1
27	1 container, 8 fluid ounces....	62	295	6	18	29	175	.1	740	.06	.27	.1	1
28	Ice milk; 1 cup, 8 fluid ounces....	67	285	9	10	42	292	.2	420	.09	.41	.2	2
	EGGS												
	Egg, raw, large:												
29	1 whole....	74	80	6	6	Trace	27	1.1	590	.05	.15	Trace	0
30	1 white....	88	15	4	Trace	Trace	3	Trace	0	Trace	.09	Trace	0
31	1 yolk....	51	60	3	5	Trace	24	.9	580	.04	.07	Trace	0
	Egg, cooked; 1 large:												
32	Boiled....	74	80	6	6	Trace	27	1.1	590	.05	.14	Trace	0
33	Scrambled (with milk and fat)....	72	110	7	8	1	51	1.1	690	.05	.18	Trace	0
	MEAT, POULTRY, FISH, SHELLFISH												
34	Bacon, broiled or fried, medium done; 2 slices....	13	95	4	9	Trace	4	.5	0	.08	.05	.8	0
	Beef, cooked, without bone:												
	Braised, simmered, or pot-roasted; 3-ounce portion:												
35	Entire portion, lean and fat....	43	340	20	28	0	9	2.6	50	.04	.15	3.1	0
36	Lean only, approx. 2 ounces....	62	115	18	4	0	8	2.2	Trace	.03	.13	2.7	0
	Hamburger patties, made with—												
37	Regular ground beef; 3-ounce patty....	54	245	21	17	0	9	2.7	30	.07	.18	4.6	0
38	Lean ground round; 3-ounce patty....	60	185	23	10	0	10	3.0	20	.08	.20	5.1	0
	Roast; 3-ounce slice from—												
	Cut having relatively large amount of fat:												
39	Entire portion, lean and fat....	35	420	15	39	0	7	2.0	80	.04	.12	2.8	0
40	Lean only, approx. 1.6												

No.		Water	Food energy	Protein	Fat	Carbo-hydrate	Calcium	Iron	Vitamin A	Thiamine	Riboflavin	Niacin	Ascorbic acid
	ounces.................	57	110	13	6	0	6	1.7	Trace	.03	.10	2.4	0
	Cut having relatively small amount of fat:												
41	Entire portion, lean and fat...	52	255	22	18	0	9	2.8	30	.06	.16	3.9	0
42	Lean only, approx. 2.3 ounces....	63	115	19	4	0	8	2.4	Trace	.05	.14	3.4	0
	Beef, cooked, without bone—Con.												
	Steak, broiled; 3-ounce portion:												
43	Entire portion, lean and fat...	39	375	19	32	0	9	2.6	60	0.06	0.16	4.0	0
44	Lean only, approx. 1.8 ounces....	59	105	17	4	0	7	2.0	Trace	.05	.13	3.3	0
	Beef, canned:												
45	Corned; 3 ounces.........	59	180	22	10	0	17	3.7	20	.01	.20	2.9	0
46	Corned beef hash; 3 ounces......	70	120	12	5	6	22	1.1	10	.02	.11	2.4	0
47	Beef, dried; 2 ounces......	48	115	19	4	0	11	2.9		.04	.18	2.2	0
48	Beef and vegetable stew; 1 cup....	79	250	13	19	17	31	2.6	2,520	.12	.15	3.4	15
	Chicken, without bone:												
49	Broiled; 3 ounces....	71	115	20	3	0	8	1.4	80	.06	.15	10.5	0
50	Canned; 3 ounces ..	62	170	25	7	0	12	1.5	160	.03	.14	5.4	0
	Chile con carne, canned:												
51	Without beans; 1 cup......	67	510	26	38	15	97	3.6	380	.05	.31	5.6	......
52	Heart, beef, trimmed of fat, braised; 3 ounces....	61	160	26	5	1	14	5.9	30	.23	1.05	6.8	3
	Lamb, cooked:												
	Chops; 1 thick chop, with bone, 4.8 ounces:												
53	Lean and fat, approx. 3.6 ounces.	44	450	24	39	0	10	2.9	......	.13	.24	5.4	0
54	Lean only, 2.4 ounces....	62	130	19	5	0	8	2.3	......	.10	.19	4.2	0
	Roast, without bone:												
	Leg; 3-ounce slice:												
55	Entire slice, lean and fat...	51	265	20	20	0	9	2.6	......	.12	.22	4.5	0
56	Lean only, approx. 2.3 ounces....	62	120	19	5	0	9	2.4	......	.11	.20	4.1	0
	Shoulder; 3-ounce portion, without bone:												
57	Entire portion, lean and fat...	48	300	18	25	0	9	2.3	......	.11	.19	4.0	0
58	Lean only, approx. 2.2 ounces....	61	125	16	6	0	7	2.1	......	.09	.17	3.5	0

Item number	Food	Water	Food energy	Protein	Fat	Total carbohydrate	Calcium	Iron	Vitamin A value	Thiamine	Riboflavin	Niacin	Ascorbic acid
59	Liver, beef, fried; 2 ounces	57	120	13	4	6	5	4.4	30,330	.15	2.25	8.4	18
60	Pork, cured, cooked: Ham, smoked; 3-ounce portion, without bone	39	340	20	28	Trace	9	2.5	0	.46	.18	3.5	0
	Luncheon meat:												
61	Boiled ham; 2 ounces	48	170	13	13	0	5	1.5	0	.57	.15	2.9	0
62	Canned, spiced; 2 ounces	55	165	8	14	1	1	1.2	0	.18	.12	1.6	0
	Pork, fresh, cooked: Chops; 1 chop, with bone, 3.5 ounces:												
63	Lean and fat, approx. 2.4 ounces	39	295	15	25	0	7	2.1	......	.60	.17	3.6	0
64	Lean only, approx. 1.6 ounces	53	120	14	7	0	6	1.8	......	.51	.15	3.1	0
65	Roast; 3-ounce slice, without bone: Entire slice, lean and fat	43	340	19	29	0	9	2.5	......	.71	.21	4.3	0
66	Simmered; 3-ounce portion, without bone: Lean only, approx. 2.2 ounces	55	160	19	9	0	8	2.4	......	.68	.20	4.1	0
67	Entire portion, lean and fat	42	355	19	30	0	9	2.4	......	.43	.20	3.9	0
68	Lean only, approx. 2 ounces	60	120	16	5	0	7	2.0	......	.37	.17	3.3	0
	Sausage:												
69	Bologna; 8 slices (4.1 by 0.1 inches each), 8 ounces	56	690	27	62	2	16	4.1	......	.36	.49	6.0	0
70	Frankfurter; 1 cooked, 1.8 ounces	58	155	6	14	1	3	.8	......	.08	.10	1.3	0
71	Pork, bulk, canned; 4 ounces	55	340	18	29	0	10	2.6	......	.23	.27	3.4	0
72	Tongue, beef, boiled or simmered; 3 ounces	61	205	18	14	Trace	7	2.5	......	.04	.26	3.1	0
73	Veal, cutlet, broiled; 3-ounce portion, without bone	60	185	23	9	0	9	2.7	......	.06	.21	4.6	0
	Fish and shellfish:												
74	Bluefish, baked or broiled; 3 ounces	68	135	22	4	0	25	.6	40	.09	.08	1.6	0
	Clams:												

No.	Food												
75	Raw, meat only; 3 ounces	80	70	11	1	3	82	6.0	90	.08	.15	1.4	0
76	Canned, solids and liquid; 3 ounces	87	45	7	1	2	74	5.4	70	.04	.08	.9	0
77	Crabmeat, canned or cooked; 3 ounces	77	90	14	2	1	38	.8	......	.04	.05	2.1	0
78	Fishsticks, breaded, cooked, frozen; 10 sticks (3.8 by 1.0 by 0.5 inches each), 8 ounces	66	400	38	20	15	25	.9	......	.09	.16	3.6	0
79	Haddock, fried; 3 ounces	67	135	16	5	6	15	.5	50	.03	.08	2.2	0
	Fish and shellfish—Continued												
	Mackerel:												
80	Broiled; 3 ounces	62	200	19	13	0	5	1.0	40	0.13	0.23	6.5	0
81	Canned, solids and liquid; 3 ounces	66	155	16	9	0	157	1.8	370	.05	.18	4.9	0
82	Ocean perch, fried (dipped in egg and bread crumbs); 3 ounces	59	195	16	11	6	14	1.3	50	.09	.10	1.7	0
83	Oysters, raw, meat only; 1 cup (13-19 medium-size oysters, selects)	85	160	20	4	8	226	13.2	740	.30	.39	6.6	0
84	Oyster stew; 1 cup (6-8 oysters)	84	200	11	12	11	269	3.3	640	.12	.40	1.7	0
85	Salmon, canned (pink); 3 ounces	70	120	17	5	0	159	.7	60	.03	.16	6.8	0
86	Sardines, canned in oil, drained solids; 3 ounces	57	180	22	9	0	367	2.5	190	.02	.18	4.6	0
87	Shad, baked; 3 ounces	64	170	20	9	0	20	2.0	20	.11	.22	7.3	......
88	Shrimp, canned, meat only; 3 ounces	66	110	23	1	......	98	2.6	50	.01	.03	1.9	0
89	Swordfish; 3 ounces	65	150	24	5	0	23	1.1	1,750	.03	.04	9.3	0
90	Tuna, canned in oil, drained solids; 3 ounces	60	170	25	7	0	7	1.2	70	.04	.10	10.9	0
	MATURE BEANS AND PEAS; NUTS												
91	Almonds, shelled; 1 cup	5	850	26	77	28	332	6.7	0	.34	1.31	5.0	Trace
	Beans, dry seed:												
	Common varieties, as Great Northern, navy, and others, canned; 1 cup:												
92	Red	76	230	15	1	42	74	4.6	0	.13	.13	1.5	Trace
	White, with tomato or molasses:												
93	With pork	69	330	16	7	54	172	4.4	140	.13	.10	1.3	5
94	Without pork	69	315	16	1	60	183	5.2	140	.13	.10	1.3	5

147

Item number	Food	Water	Food energy	Protein	Fat	Total carbohydrate	Calcium	Iron	Vitamin A value	Thiamine	Ribo-flavin	Niacin	Ascorbic acid
95	Lima, cooked; 1 cup	64	260	16	1	48	56	5.6	Trace	.26	.12	1.3	Trace
96	Brazil nuts, broken pieces; 1 cup	5	905	20	92	15	260	4.8	Trace	1.21	.....	1.9	.....
97	Cashew nuts, roasted; 1 cup	5	770	25	65	35	51	5.1	.....	.49	.46	.....	.....
98	Coconut; 1 cup: Fresh, shredded	50	330	3	31	13	15	1.7	0	.06	.03	.5	4
99	Dried, shredded (sweetened)	3	345	2	24	33	13	1.6	0	.04	.02	.4	0
100	Cowpeas or black-eyed peas, dry, cooked; 1 cup	80	190	13	1	34	42	3.2	20	.41	.11	1.1	Trace
101	Peanuts, roasted, shelled; 1 cup	2	840	39	71	28	104	3.2	0	.47	.19	24.6	0
102	Peanut butter; 1 tablespoon	2	90	4	8	3	12	.4	0	.02	.02	2.8	0
103	Peas, split, dry, cooked; 1 cup	70	290	20	1	52	28	4.2	120	.36	.22	2.2	Trace
104	Pecans, halves; 1 cup	3	740	10	77	16	79	2.6	140	.93	.14	1.0	2
105	Walnuts, shelled; 1 cup: Black or native, chopped	3	790	26	75	19	Trace	7.6	380	.28	.14	.9	.....
106	English or Persian, halves	4	650	15	64	16	99	3.1	30	.33	.13	.9	3
	VEGETABLES												
107	Asparagus: Cooked; 1 cup	92	35	4	Trace	6	33	1.8	1,820	.23	.30	2.1	40
108	Canned; 6 medium-size spears: Green	92	20	2	Trace	3	18	1.8	770	.06	.08	.9	17
109	Bleached	92	20	2	Trace	4	15	1.0	70	.05	.07	.8	17
110	Beans: Lima, immature, cooked; 1 cup	75	150	8	1	29	46	2.7	460	.22	.14	1.8	24
111	Snap, green: Cooked; 1 cup: In small amount of water, short time	92	25	2	Trace	6	45	.9	830	.09	.12	.6	18
112	In large amount of water, long time	92	25	2	Trace	6	45	.9	830	.06	.11	.5	12
113	Canned: Solids and liquid; 1 cup	94	45	2	Trace	10	65	3.3	990	.08	.10	.7	9
114	Strained or chopped; 1												

No.	Food, approximate measure, and weight	Water (%)	Food energy (cal.)	Protein (g)	Fat (g)	Carbohydrate (g)	Calcium (mg)	Iron (mg)	Vitamin A (I.U.)	Thiamine (mg)	Riboflavin (mg)	Niacin (mg)	Ascorbic acid (mg)
115	Beets, cooked, diced; 1 cup............	93	70	2	Trace	16	34	0.7	30	.03	.07	.4	11
116	Broccoli, cooked, flower stalks; 1 cup...	88	45	5	Trace	8	195	1.2	5,100	.10	.22	1.2	111
117	Brussels sprouts, cooked; 1 cup........	90	60	6	Trace	12	44	2.0	520	.08	.16	.6	61
	Cabbage; 1 cup:												
118	Raw, finely shredded................	92	25	1	Trace	5	46	.5	80	.05	.05	.3	50
119	Raw, coleslaw.....................	84	100	2	7	9	47	.5	80	.05	.05	.3	50
	Cabbage; 1 cup—Con.												
	Cooked:												
120	In small amount of water, short time...	92	40	2	Trace	9	78	0.8	150	0.08	0.08	0.5	53
121	In large amount of water, long time...	92	40	2	Trace	9	78	.8	150	.05	.05	.3	32
	Cabbage, celery or Chinese; 1 cup:												
122	Raw, leaves and stem (1-inch pieces)...	95	15	1	Trace	2	43	.9	260	.03	.04	.4	31
123	Cooked..........................	95	25	2	1	5	82	1.7	490	.04	.06	.6	42
	Carrots:												
124	Raw; 1 carrot (5½ by 1 inch) or 25 thin strips...............	88	20	1	Trace	5	20	.4	6,000	.03	.03	.3	3
125	Raw, grated; 1 cup...............	88	45	1	Trace	10	43	.9	13,200	.06	.06	.7	7
126	Cooked, diced; 1 cup............	92	45	1	Trace	9	38	.9	18,130	.07	.07	.7	6
127	Canned, strained or chopped; 1 ounce..........................	92	5	Trace	Trace	2	7	.2	3,400	.01	.01	.1	1
128	Cauliflower, cooked, flower buds; 1 cup.	92	30	3	Trace	6	26	1.3	110	.07	.10	.6	34
	Celery, raw:												
129	Large stalk, 8 inches long...........	94	5	Trace	Trace	2	20	.2	0	.02	.02	.2	3
130	Diced; 1 cup....................	94	20	1	Trace	6	50	.5	0	.05	.04	.4	7
131	Collards, cooked; 1 cup............	87	75	7	1	14	473	3.0	14,500	.15	.46	3.2	84
	Corn, sweet:												
132	Cooked; 1 ear 5 inches long.......	76	65	2	1	16	4	.5	310	.09	.08	1.1	6
133	Canned, solids and liquid; 1 cup...	80	170	5	1	41	10	1.3	520	.07	.13	2.4	14
134	Cowpeas, immature seeds, cooked; 1 cup.	75	150	11	1	25	59	4.0	620	.46	.13	1.3	32
135	Cucumbers, raw, pared; 6 slices (⅛-inch thick, center section).......	96	5	Trace	Trace	1	5	.2	0	.02	.02	.1	4
136	Dandelion greens, cooked; 1 cup...	86	80	5	1	16	337	5.6	27,310	.23	.22	1.3	29
137	Endive, curly (including escarole); 2 ounces..........................	93	10	1	Trace	2	45	1.0	1,700	.04	.07	.2	6
138	Kale, cooked; 1 cup................	87	45	4	1	8	248	2.4	9,220	.08	.25	1.9	56

Item number	Food	Water	Food energy	Protein	Fat	Total carbohydrate	Calcium	Iron	Vitamin A value	Thiamine	Riboflavin	Niacin	Ascorbic acid
	Lettuce, headed, raw:												
139	2 large or 4 small leaves	95	5	1	Trace	1	11	.2	270	.02	.04	.1	4
140	1 compact head (4¾-inch diameter)	95	70	5	1	13	100	2.3	2,470	.20	.38	.9	35
141	Mushrooms, canned, solids and liquid; 1 cup	93	30	3	Trace	9	17	2.0		.02	.60	4.8	
142	Mustard greens, cooked; 1 cup	92	30	3	Trace	6	308	4.1	10,050	.04	.25	1.0	63
143	Okra, cooked; 8 pods (3 inches long, ⅝-inch diameter)	90	30	2	Trace	6	70	.6	630	.08	.05	.7	17
	Onions:												
	Mature:												
144	Raw; 1 onion (2½-inch diameter)	88	50	2	Trace	11	35	.6	60	.04	.04	.2	10
145	Cooked; 1 cup	90	80	Trace	Trace	18	67	1.0	110	.04	.06	.4	13
146	Young green; 6 small, without tops	88	25	Trace	Trace	5	68	.4	30	.02	.02	.1	12
147	Parsley, raw; 1 tablespoon chopped	84	1	Trace	Trace	Trace	7	.2	290	Trace	.01	.3	7
148	Parsnips, cooked; 1 cup	84	95	2	1	22	88	1.1	0	.09	.16		19
	Peas, green; 1 cup:												
149	Cooked	82	110	8	1	19	35	3.0	1,150	.40	.22	3.7	24
150	Canned, solids and liquid	82	170	8	1	32	62	4.5	1,350	.28	.15	2.6	21
151	Canned, strained; 1 ounce	86	10	1	Trace	2	5	.3	160	.03	.02	.3	2
	Peppers, sweet:												
152	Green, raw; 1 medium	93	15	1	Trace	3	6	.4	260	.05	.05	.3	79
153	Red, raw; 1 medium	91	20	1	Trace	4	8	.4	2,670	.05	.05	.3	122
154	Pimientos, canned; 1 medium	92	10	Trace	Trace	2	3	.6	870	.01	.02	.1	36
155	Peppers, hot, red, without seeds, dried, ground (chili powder); 1 tablespoon	13	50	2	1	9	20	1.2	11,520	.03	.20	1.6	2
	Potatoes:												
156	Baked or boiled; 1 medium, 2½-inch diameter (weight raw, about 5 ounces): Baked in jacket	75	90	3	Trace	21	9	.7	Trace	.10	.04	1.7	20
157	Boiled; peeled before boiling	80	90	3	Trace	21	9	.7	Trace	.11	.04	1.4	20
158	Chips; 10 medium (2-inch diameter)	3	110	1	7	10	6	.4	Trace	.04	.02	.6	2

French fried:

No.	Food												
159	Frozen, ready to be heated for serving; 10 pieces (2 by ½ by ¾ inch)	64	95	2	4	15	4	.8	Trace	.08	.01	1.2	10
160	Ready-to-eat, deep fat for entire process; 10 pieces (2 by ½ by ¾ inch)	45	155	2	7	20	9	.7	Trace	.06	.04	1.8	8

[1] Vitamin A based on yellow corn; white corn contains only a trace

Potatoes—Con.

Mashed; 1 cup:

No.	Food												
161	Milk added	80	145	4	1	30	47	1.0	50	0.17	0.11	0.2	17
162	Milk and butter added	76	230	4	12	28	45	1.0	470	.16	.10	1.6	16
163	Pumpkin, canned; 1 cup	90	75	2	Trace	18	46	1.6	7,750	.04	.14	1.2	.....
164	Radishes, raw; 4 small	94	10	Trace	Trace	2	15	.4	10	.01	.01	.1	10
165	Sauerkraut, canned, drained solids; 1 cup	91	30	2	Trace	7	54	.8	60	.05	.10	.2	24

Spinach:

No.	Food												
166	Cooked; 1 cup	91	45	6	1	6	223	3.6	21,200	.14	.36	1.1	54
167	Canned, creamed, strained; 1 ounce	90	10	1	Trace	2	19	.3	750	.01	.03	.1	1

Squash:

Cooked, 1 cup:

No.	Food												
168	Summer, diced	95	35	1	1	8	32	.8	550	.08	.15	1.3	23
169	Winter, baked, mashed	86	95	4	1	23	49	1.6	12,690	.10	.31	1.2	14
170	Canned, strained or chopped; 1 ounce	92	10	Trace	Trace	2	7	.1	510	.01	.01	.1	1

Sweetpotatoes:

Baked or boiled; 1 medium, 5 by 2 inches (weight raw, about 6 ounces):

No.	Food												
171	Baked in jacket	64	155	2	1	36	44	1.0	[1]8,970	.10	.07	.7	24
172	Boiled in jacket	71	170	2	1	39	47	1.0	[1]11,610	.13	.09	.9	25
173	Candied; 1 small, 3½ by 2 inches	60	295	2	6	60	65	1.6	[1]11,030	.10	.08	.8	17
174	Canned, vacuum or solid pack; 1 cup	72	235	4	Trace	54	54	1.7	17,110	.12	.09	1.1	30

Tomatoes:

No.	Food												
175	Raw; 1 medium (2 by 2½ inches), about ⅓ pound	94	30	2	Trace	6	16	.9	1,640	.08	.06	.8	35
176	Canned or cooked; 1 cup	94	45	2	Trace	9	27	1.5	2,540	.14	.08	1.7	40
177	Tomato juice, canned; 1 cup	94	50	2	Trace	10	17	1.0	2,540	.12	.07	1.8	38
178	Tomato catsup; 1 tablespoon	70	15	Trace	Trace	4	2	.1	320	.02	.01	.4	2

151

Item number	Food	Water	Food energy	Protein	Fat	Total carbohydrate	Calcium	Iron	Vitamin A value	Thiamine	Riboflavin	Niacin	Ascorbic acid
179	Turnips, cooked, diced; 1 cup............	92	40	1	Trace	9	62	.8	Trace	.06	.09	.6	28
180	Turnip greens, cooked; 1 cup............	90	45	4	1	8	376	3.5	15,370	.09	.59	1.0	87
	FRUITS												
181	Apples, raw; 1 medium (2½ inch diameter), about ⅓ pound............	85	70	Trace	Trace	18	8	.4	50	.04	.02	.1	3
182	Apple betty; 1 cup............	64	350	4	8	69	41	1.4	270	.13	.10	.9	Trace
183	Apple juice, fresh or canned; 1 cup............	86	125	Trace	0	34	15	1.2	90	.05	.07	Trace	2
	Apple sauce, canned:												
184	Sweetened; 1 cup............	80	185	Trace	Trace	50	10	1.0	80	.05	.03	.1	3
185	Unsweetened; 1 cup............	88	100	Trace	Trace	26	10	1.0	70	.05	.02	.1	3
186	Apricots, raw; 3 apricots (about ⅓ pound)............	85	55	1	Trace	14	18	.5	2,890	.03	.04	.7	10
	Apricots, canned:												
187	Heavy sirup pack, halves and sirup; 1 cup............	78	200	1	Trace	54	34	1.0	4,070	.05	.07	1.1	10
188	Water pack, halves and liquid; 1 cup............	90	80	1	Trace	21	27	.7	3,320	.04	.05	.9	8
	Apricots, dried:												
189	Uncooked; 1 cup (40 halves, small)............	25	390	8	1	100	100	8.2	16,390	.02	.24	4.9	19
190	Cooked unsweetened, fruit and liquid; 1 cup............	76	240	5	1	62	63	5.1	10,130	.01	.13	2.8	8
191	Apricots and applesauce, canned, strained or chopped; 1 ounce............	80	20	Trace	Trace	5	3	.2	440	.01	.01	.1	Trace
192	Apricot nectar; 1 cup............	85	135	1	Trace	36	22	.5	2,380	.02	.02	.5	7
	Avocados, raw, California varieties (mainly Fuerte):												
193	1 cup (½-inch cubes)............	74	260	3	26	9	15	.9	430	.16	.30	2.4	21
194	⅜ of a 10-ounce avocado (3½ by 3¼ inches)............	74	185	2	18	6	11	.6	310	.12	.21	1.7	15
	Avocados, raw, Florida varieties:												
195	1 cup (½ inch cubes)............	78	195	2	17	13	15	.9	430	.16	.30	2.4	21

No.	Food												
196	½ of a 13-ounce avocado (4 by 3 inches)	78	160	2	14	11	12	.7	350	.13	.24	2.0	17
197	Bananas, raw; 1 medium (6 by 1¼ inches), about ½ pound	76	85	1	Trace	23	10	.7	170	.05	.06	.7	10
198	Blackberries, raw; 1 cup	85	80	2	1	18	46	1.3	280	.05	.06	.5	30
199	Blueberries, raw; 1 cup	83	85	1	1	21	22	1.1	400	.04	.03	.4	23
200	Cantaloups, raw; ½ melon (5-inch diameter)	94	40	1	Trace	9	33	0.8	[3]6,590	0.09	0.07	1.0	63
201	Cherries, sour, sweet, and hybrid, raw; 1 cup	83	65	1	1	15	19	.4	650	.05	.06	.4	9
	Cherries, canned:												
202	Red sour, pitted; 1 cup	87	120	2	1	30	28	.8	1,840	.07	.04	.4	14
203	Cranberry juice cocktail, canned; 1 cup	85	135	Trace	Trace	36	10	.5	20	.02	.02	.1	5
204	Cranberry sauce, sweetened; 1 cup	48	550	Trace	1	142	22	.8	80	.06	.06	.3	5
205	Dates, "fresh" and dried, pitted and cut; 1 cup	20	505	4	1	134	103	5.3	170	.16	.17	3.9	0
	Figs:												
206	Raw; 3 small (1½-inch diameter), about ¼ pound	78	90	2	Trace	22	62	.7	90	.06	.06	.6	2
207	Dried; 1 large (2 by 1 inch)	23	60	1	Trace	15	43	.3	20	.02	.02	.2	0
208	Fruit cocktail, canned in heavy sirup, solids and liquid; 1 cup	81	175	Trace	Trace	47	23	1.0	360	.04	.03	1.1	5
	Grapefruit:												
	Raw; ½ medium (4¼-inch diameter, No. 64's):												
209	White	89	50	1	Trace	14	21	.5	10	.05	.02	.2	50
210	Pink or red	89	55	1	Trace	14	21	.5	590	.05	.02	.3	48
211	Raw, sections, white; 1 cup	89	75	1	Trace	20	31	.8	20	.07	.03	.3	72
	Canned:												
212	Sirup pack, solids and liquid; 1 cup	81	165	1	Trace	44	32	.7	20	.07	.04	.5	75
213	Water pack, solids and liquid; 1 cup	91	70	1	Trace	18	31	.7	20	.07	.04	.5	72
	Grapefruit juice:												
214	Raw; 1 cup	90	85	1	Trace	23	22	.5	[4]20	.09	.04	.5	92
	Canned:												
215	Unsweetened; 1 cup	89	95	1	Trace	24	20	1.0	20	.07	.04	.4	84
216	Sweetened; 1 cup	86	120	1	Trace	32	20	1.0	20	.07	.04	.4	78

[3] Average vitamin A value for important commercial varieties. Varieties with pale flesh contain very small amounts while those with deep orange-colored flesh have much higher contents than the value shown in the table.

Item number	Food	Water	Food energy	Protein	Fat	Total carbohydrate	Calcium	Iron	Vitamin A value	Thiamine	Riboflavin	Niacin	Ascorbic acid
	Frozen concentrate, unsweetened:												
217	Undiluted; 1 can (6 fluid ounces).	62	280	4	1	72	70	.8	60	.29	.12	1.4	286
218	Diluted, ready-to-serve; 1 cup.	89	95	1	Trace	24	25	.2	20	.10	.04	.5	96
	Frozen concentrate, sweetened:												
219	Undiluted; 1 can (6 fluid ounces).	57	320	3	1	85	59	.6	50	.24	.11	1.2	245
220	Diluted, ready-to-serve; 1 cup. .	88	105	1	Trace	28	20	.2	20	.08	.03	.4	82
	Dehydrated:												
221	Crystals; 1 can (net weight 4 ounces)	1	400	5	—	103	99	1.1	90	.41	.18	2.0	399
222	With water added, ready-to-serve; 1 cup.	90	90	1	Trace	24	22	.2	20	.10	.05	.5	92
	Grapes, raw; 1 cup:												
223	American type (slip skin)	82	70	1	1	16	13	.4	100	.05	.03	.3	4
224	European type (adherent skin)	81	100	1	Trace	26	18	.6	150	.08	.04	.4	7
225	Grape juice, bottled; 1 cup	82	165	1	1	42	25	.8	....	.11	.06	.7	Trace
	Lemon juice:												
226	Raw; 1 cup	91	60	1	Trace	20	27	.5	Trace	.08	.03	.3	129
227	Canned; 1 cup	91	60	1	Trace	20	27	.5	Trace	.07	.03	.3	102
	Lemonade concentrate, frozen, sweetened:												
228	Undiluted; 1 can (6 fluid ounces) . .	48	305	1	Trace	113	9	.4	Trace	.05	.06	.7	67
229	Diluted, ready-to-serve; 1 cup	88	75	Trace	Trace	28	2	.1	Trace	.01	.01	.2	17
	Lime juice:												
230	Raw; 1 cup.	90	65	1	Trace	22	22	1.5	Trace	.03	.04	.4	80
231	Canned; 1 cup.	90	65	1	Trace	22	22	1.5	Trace	.02	.04	.4	52
	Limeade concentrate, frozen, sweetened:												
232	Undiluted; 1 can (6 fluid ounces). .	50	295	Trace	Trace	109	11	.7	Trace	.01	.02	.2	262
233	Diluted, ready-to-serve; 1 cup. .	90	75	Trace	Trace	27	2	.2	Trace	Trace	.01	.1	6
	Oranges, raw; 1 large orange (3-inch diameter):												
234	Navel.	86	70	2	Trace	17	48	.3	270	.11	.03	.4	83
235	Other varieties.	86	70	1	Trace	18	63	.3	290	.12	.03	.4	66
	Orange juice: Raw; 1 cup:												
236	California (Valencias).	88	105	2	Trace	26	37	.5	500	.20	.05	.6	126

No.	Food, approximate measure, and weight	Water (%)	Food energy (cal.)	Protein (g)	Fat (g)	Carbohydrate (g)	Calcium (mg)	Iron (mg)	Vitamin A (I.U.)	Thiamine (mg)	Riboflavin (mg)	Niacin (mg)	Ascorbic acid (mg)
	Florida varieties:												
237	Early and midseason.....	90	90	1	Trace	23	25	.5	490	.20	.05	.6	127
238	Late season (Valencias).....	88	105	1	Trace	26	25	.5	500	.20	.05	.6	92
239	Canned, unsweetened; 1 cup.....	87	110	2	Trace	28	25	1.0	500	.17	.05	.6	100
	Orange juice—Con.												
	Frozen concentrate:												
240	Undiluted; 1 can (6 fl. ounces).	58	305	5	Trace	80	69	0.8	1,490	0.63	0.10	2.4	332
241	Diluted, ready-to-serve; 1 cup.	88	105	2	Trace	27	22	.2	500	.21	.03	.8	112
	Dehydrated:												
242	Crystals; 1 can (net weight 4 ounces).....	1	395	6	2	100	95	1.9	1,900	.76	.19	2.5	406
243	With water added, ready-to-serve; 1 cup.....	88	105	1	Trace	27	25	.5	500	.20	.05	.6	108
	Orange and grapefruit juice, frozen concentrate:												
244	Undiluted; 1 can (6 fluid ounces).....	59	300	4	1	78	61	.8	790	.47	.06	2.3	301
245	Diluted, ready-to-serve; 1 cup.....	88	100	1	Trace	26	20	.2	270	.16	.02	.8	102
	Peaches:												
	Raw:												
246	1 medium (2½ by 2-inch diameter), about ¼ pound.....	89	35	1	Trace	10	9	.5	⁵1,320	.02	.05	1.0	7
247	1 cup, sliced.....	89	65	1	Trace	16	15	.8	⁵2,230	.03	.08	1.6	12
	Canned (yellow-fleshed) solids and liquid:												
248	Heavy-syrup pack; 1 cup.....	80	185	1	Trace	49	13	.8	1,000	.02	.06	1.3	8
249	Water pack; 1 cup.....	92	65	1	Trace	17	15	.7	1,100	.02	.07	1.4	9
250	Strained; 1 ounce.....	82	20	Trace	Trace	5	2	.2	150	Trace	.01	.2	Trace
	Dried:												
251	Uncooked; 1 cup.....	25	420	5	1	109	80	9.6	6,330	.02	.32	8.4	32
252	Cooked, unsweetened; 1 cup (10-12 halves and 6 tablespoons liquid).....	77	220	3	1	58	43	5.1	3,350	.01	.16	4.1	6
	Frozen:												
253	1 12-ounce carton.....	79	265	1	Trace	69	20	1.4	1,770	.04	.10	1.8	⁶99
254	1 16-ounce can.....	79	335	2	Trace	92	27	1.8	2,360	.05	.14	2.4	⁶132
255	Peach nectar, canned; 1 cup.....	87	115	Trace	Trace	31	10	.5	1,070	.02	.05	1.0	1

⁵ Vitamin A based on deeply colored varieties.
⁴ Vitamin A value for juice from white grapefruit. The vitamin A value per cup of juice from pink or red grapefruit is 1,080 I.U.

Item number	Food	Water	Food energy	Protein	Fat	Total carbohydrate	Calcium	Iron	Vitamin A value	Thiamine	Riboflavin	Niacin	Ascorbic acid
	Pears:												
256	Raw; 1 pear (3- by 2½-inch diameter)	83	100	1	1	25	13	.5	30	.04	.07	.2	7
	Canned, solids and liquid:												
257	Heavy-sirup pack; 1 cup	81	175	1	Trace	47	18	1.3	Trace	.02	.05	.4	3
258	Strained; 1 ounce	84	15	Trace	Trace	4	3	.1	Trace	Trace	Trace	.1	Trace
259	Pear nectar, canned; 1 cup	86	125	1	Trace	33	8	.2	10	.01	.01	.05	1
	Pineapple:												
260	Raw, diced; 1 cup	85	75	1	Trace	19	22	.4	180	.12	.04	.04	33
	Canned:												
	Sirup pack, solids and liquid:												
261	Crushed; 1 cup	78	205	1	Trace	55	75	1.6	210	.20	.20	.04	23
262	Sliced; 2 small or 1 large slice and 2 tablespoons juice	78	95	Trace	Trace	26	35	.7	100	.09	.09	.02	11
263	Pineapple juice, canned; 1 cup	86	120	1	Trace	32	37	1.2	200	.13	.13	.04	22
	Plums:												
264	Raw; 1 plum (2-inch diameter), about 2 ounces	86	30	Trace	Trace	7	10	.3	200	.04	.04	.02	3
	Canned (Italian prunes):												
265	Sirup pack, solids and liquid; 1 cup	79	185	1	Trace	50	20	2.7	560	.07	.07	.06	3
	Prunes, dried:												
266	Uncooked; 4 medium prunes	24	70	1	Trace	19	14	1.0	430	.02	.02	.05	1
267	Cooked, unsweetened; 1 cup (17–18 prunes and ⅓ cup liquid)	65	295	3	1	78	57	4.3	1,780	.08	.08	.18	3
268	Canned, strained; 1 ounce	73	25	Trace	Trace	7	8	.4	170	.01	.01	.01	1
269	Prune juice, canned; 1 cup	80	170	1	Trace	45	36	10.6		.01	.03	1.1	4
270	Raisins, dried; 1 cup	18	460	4	Trace	124	99	6.2	30	.13	.13	.7	2
	Raspberries, red:												
271	Raw; 1 cup	84	70	1	Trace	17	49	1.1	160	.03	.03	.08	29
272	Frozen; 10-ounce carton	74	280	2	1	70	79	1.7	220	.03	.03	.12	45
273	Rhubarb, cooked, sugar added; 1 cup	63	385	1	Trace	98	112	1.1	70	.02	.02		17
	Strawberries:												
274	Raw; 1 cup	90	55	1	1	12	42	1.2	90	.04	.04	.10	89
275	Frozen; 10-ounce carton	72	300	2	1	75	62	1.7	120	.05	.05	.14	116

477248°—59——18

No.	Food and measure												
276	Frozen; 16-ounce can	72	485	3	2	121	100	2.7	190	.08	.23	.8	186
277	Tangerines; 1 medium (2½-inch diameter), about ¼ pound	87	40	1	Trace	10	34	.3	360	.05	.01	.1	26
278	Tangerine juice: Canned; 1 cup	89	100	1	Trace	25	45	.5	1,050	.14	.04	.3	56
279	Frozen concentrate: Undiluted; 6-fluid-ounce can	58	315	4	1	80	130	1.5	3,070	.43	.12	.9	202
280	Diluted, ready-to-serve; 1 cup	88	105	1	Trace	27	45	.5	1,020	.14	.04	.3	67
281	Watermelon; 1 wedge (4 by 8 inches), about 2 pounds (weighed with rind)	92	120	2	1	29	30	.9	2,530	.20	.22	.7	26

GRAIN PRODUCTS

No.	Food and measure												
282	Biscuits, baking powder, enriched flour; 1 biscuit (2½-inch diameter)	27	130	3	4	20	83	.7	0	.09	.08	.7	0
283	Bran flakes (40 percent bran) with added thiamine; 1 ounce	4	85	3	1	22	17	1.1	0	.13	.07	2.5	0
	Breads: Cracked wheat:												
284	1 pound (20 slices)	35	1,190	39	10	236	399	5.0	Trace	.53	.42	5.8	Trace
285	1 slice (½ inch thick)	35	60	2	1	12	20	.3	Trace	.03	.02	.3	Trace
	French or vienna:												
286	Enriched; 1 pound	31	1,315	41	14	251	195	10.0	Trace	1.26	.98	11.3	Trace
287	Unenriched; 1 pound	31	1,315	41	14	251	195	3.2	Trace	.39	.39	3.6	Trace
	Italian:												
288	Enriched; 1 pound	32	1,250	41	4	256	77	10.0	0	1.31	.93	11.7	0
289	Unenriched; 1 pound	32	1,250	41	4	256	77	3.2	0	.39	.27	3.6	0
	Raisin:												
290	1 pound (20 slices)	35	1,190	30	13	243	322	5.9	Trace	.24	.42	3.0	Trace
291	1 slice (½ inch thick)	35	60	2	1	12	16	.3	Trace	.01	.02	.2	Trace
	Rye: American (light):												
292	1 pound (20 slices)	36	1,100	41	5	236	340	7.3	0	.81	.33	6.4	0
293	1 slice (½ inch thick)	36	55	2	Trace	12	17	.4	0	.04	.02	.3	0
	Pumpernickel:												
294	1 pound	34	1,115	41	5	241	381	10.9	0	1.05	.63	5.4	0

[5] Vitamin A value of yellow-fleshed varieties; the value is negligible in white-fleshed varieties.

[6] Content of frozen peaches with added ascorbic acid; when not added the content is 14 milligrams per 12-ounce carton and 18 milligrams per 16-ounce can.

Item number	Food	Water	Food energy	Protein	Fat	Total carbohydrate	Calcium	Iron	Vitamin A value	Thiamine	Riboflavin	Niacin	Ascorbic acid
	White:[7]												
	Enriched, made with—												
	1-2 percent nonfat dry milk:												
295	1 pound (20 slices).........	36	1,225	39	15	229	318	10.9	Trace	1.13	.77	10.4	Trace
296	1 slice (½ inch thick).....	36	60	2	1	12	16	.6	Trace	.06	.04	.5	Trace
	3-4 percent nonfat dry milk:												
297	1 pound (20 slices).........	36	1,225	39	15	229	381	11.3	Trace	1.13	.95	10.8	Trace
298	1 slice (½ inch thick).....	36	60	2	1	12	19	.6	Trace	.06	.05	.6	Trace
	5-6 percent nonfat dry milk:												
299	1 pound (20 slices).........	35	1,245	41	17	228	435	11.3	Trace	1.22	.91	11.0	Trace
300	1 slice (½ inch thick).....	35	65	2	1	12	22	.6	Trace	.06	.05	.6	Trace
	Unenriched, made with—												
	1-2 percent nonfat dry milk:												
301	1 pound (20 slices).........	36	1,225	39	15	229	318	3.2	Trace	.40	.36	5.6	Trace
302	1 slice (½ inch thick).....	36	60	2	1	12	16	.2	Trace	.02	.02	.3	Trace
	3-4 percent nonfat dry milk:												
303	1 pound (20 slices).........	36	1,225	39	15	229	381	3.2	Trace	.31	.39	5.0	Trace
304	1 slice (½ inch thick).....	36	60	2	1	12	19	.2	Trace	.02	.02	.3	Trace
	5-6 percent nonfat dry milk:												
305	1 pound (20 slices).........	35	1,245	41	17	228	435	3.2	Trace	.32	.59	4.1	Trace
306	1 slice (½ inch thick).....	35	65	2	1	12	22	.2	Trace	.02	.03	.2	Trace
	Whole wheat, graham, or entire wheat:												
307	1 pound (20 slices).........	36	1,105	48	14	216	449	10.4	Trace	1.17	1.03	12.9	Trace
308	1 slice (½ inch thick).....	36	55	2	1	11	23	.5	Trace	.06	.05	.7	Trace
	Cakes:												
309	Angelfood; 2-inch sector (1/12 of cake, 8-inch diameter).....	32	110	3	Trace	23	2	.1	0	Trace	.05	.1	0
	Butter cakes:												
	Plain cake and cupcakes without icing:												
310	1 square (3 by 2 by 1½ inches).....	27	180	4	5	31	85	.2	[8]70	.02	.05	.2	0
311	1 cupcake (2¾-inch diameter).....	27	130	3	3	23	62	.2	[8]50	.01	.03	.1	0

No.	Food												
312	Plain cake with icing: 2-inch sector of iced layer cake (1/16 of cake, 10-inch diameter)	25	320	6	6	62	117	.4	[8]90	.02	.07	.2	0
313	Rich cake: 2-inch sector of layer cake, iced (1/16 of cake, 10-inch diameter)	21	490	6	19	76	114	0.6	[8]220	0.03	0.10	0.2	0
314	Fruit cake, dark; 1 piece (2 by 2 by ½ inches)	23	105	2	4	17	29	.8	[8]50	.04	.04	.3	0
315	Gingerbread; 1 piece (2 by 2 by 2 inches)	30	180	2	7	28	63	1.4	50	.02	.05	.6	0
316	Sponge; 2-inch sector (1/12 of cake, 8-inch diameter)	32	115	3	2	22	11	.6	210	.02	.06	.1	0
317	Cookies, plain and assorted; 1 cookie (3-inch diameter)	5	110	1	3	19	6	.2	0	.01	.01	.1	0
318	Cornbread or muffins made with enriched, degermed cornmeal; 1 muffin (2¾-inch diameter)	49	105	3	2	18	67	.9	[9]60	.08	.11	.6	0
319	Corn, puffed, presweetened, added thiamine, riboflavin, niacin, and iron; 1 ounce	3	110	1	Trace	26	3	.5	......	.12	.05	.5	0
320	Corn and soy shreds, added thiamine and niacin; 1 ounce	4	100	5	Trace	21	24	1.2	......	.19	.04	1.2	0
321	Corn cereal mixture (mainly degermed cornmeal) puffed, added thiamine, niacin, and iron; 1 ounce	3	115	2	1	23	6	1.2	......	.15	.04	.6	0
322	Cornflakes: With added thiamine, niacin, and iron; 1 ounce	4	110	2	Trace	24	3	.5	0	.12	.03	.6	0
323	Presweetened, added thiamine, niacin, and iron; 1 ounce	4	110	1	Trace	26	1	.5	0	.12	.01	.6	0
324	Corn grits, degermed, cooked: Enriched; 1 cup	87	120	3	Trace	27	2	.7	[10]100	.11	.08	1.0	0

7 The amount of nonfat dry milk in commercial bread is unknown; use bread made with 3-4 percent nonfat dry milk.

8 If the fat used in the recipe were butter or fortified margarine, the vitamin A value for plain cake would be 200 I.U. per large square, item 310; 280 I.U. per cupcake, item 311; 900 I.U. per 2-inch sector, iced, item 312; for rich cake, 900 I.U. per 2-inch sector, iced, item 313; for fruit cake

150 I.U. per cupcake, item 311; 280 I.U. per 2-inch sector, iced, item 312; 900 I.U. per 2-inch sector, iced, item 313; for fruit cake

120 I.U. per piece (2 by 2 by ½ inches), item 314.

Item number	Food	Water	Food energy	Protein	Fat	Total carbohydrate	Calcium	Iron	Vitamin A value	Thiamine	Riboflavin	Niacin	Ascorbic acid
325	Unenriched; 1 cup...............	87	120	3	Trace	27	2	.2	10 100	.04	.01	.4	0
	Crackers:												
326	Graham; 4 small or 2 medium....	6	55	1	1	10	3	.3	0	.04	.02	.2	0
327	Saltines; 2 crackers (2-inch square).	5	35	1	1	6	2	.1	0	Trace	Trace	.1	0
	Soda, plain:												
328	2 crackers (2½-inch square).....	6	45	1	1	8	2	.1	0	.01	.01	.1	0
329	10 oyster crackers or 1 tablespoon cracker meal.....	6	45	1	1	7	2	.1	0	.01	Trace	.1	0
330	Doughnuts, cake type; 1 doughnut.....	19	135	2	7	17	23	.4	40	.05	.04	.4	0
331	Farina, enriched to minimum levels for required nutrients and for the optional nutrient, calcium; cooked; 1 cup:	89	105	3	Trace	22	31	.8	0	.11	.07	1.0	0
	Macaroni, cooked; 1 cup:												
	Enriched:												
332	Cooked 8–10 minutes (undergoes additional cooking as ingredient of a food mixture).....	64	190	6	1	39	14	1.4	0	.23	.14	1.9	0
333	Cooked until tender...........	72	155	5	1	32	11	1.3	0	.19	.11	1.5	0
	Unenriched:												
334	Cooked 8–10 minutes (undergoes additional cooking as ingredient of a food mixture).....	64	190	6	1	39	14	.6	0	.02	.02	.5	0
335	Cooked until tender..........	72	155	5	1	32	11	.6	0	.02	.02	.4	0
336	Macaroni and cheese, baked (enriched macaroni used); 1 cup...........	58	475	18	25	44	394	2.0	970	.22	.46	1.9	Trace
337	Muffins, made with enriched white flour; 1 muffin (2¾-inch diameter).........	37	135	4	4	20	99	.8	50	.09	.10	.7	0
	Noodles (egg noodles), cooked:												
338	Enriched; 1 cup...........	70	200	7	2	37	16	1.4	60	.23	.14	1.8	0
339	Unenriched; 1 cup...........	70	200	7	2	37	16	1.0	60	.04	.03	.7	0
340	Oat cereal (mixture, mainly oat flour), ready-to-eat, added B vitamins and minerals; 1 ounce....	3	115	4	2	21	45	1.2	0	.22	.04	.5	0

341	Oatmeal or rolled oats, regular or quick cooking, cooked; 1 cup..........	85	150	5	2	26	21	1.7	0	.22	.05	.4	0
	Pancakes, baked; 1 cake (4-inch diameter):												
342	Wheat (home recipe)..........	55	60	2	2	7	43	0.2	50	0.02	0.03	0.1	Trace
343	Buckwheat (with buckwheat pancake mix)	62	45	2	2	6	67	.3	30	.04	.04	.2	Trace
	Pies; 4-inch sector (⅓ of 9-inch diameter pie):												
344	Apple..........	48	330	3	13	53	9	.5	220	.04	.02	.3	1
345	Cherry..........	46	340	3	13	55	14	.6	520	.04	.02	.3	2
346	Custard..........	58	265	7	11	34	162	1.6	290	.07	.21	.4	0
347	Lemon meringue..........	47	300	4	12	45	24	.6	210	.04	.10	.2	1
348	Mince..........	43	340	3	9	62	22	3.0	10	.09	.05	.5	1
349	Pumpkin..........	59	265	5	12	34	70	1.0	2,480	.04	.15	.4	0
350	Pretzels; 5 small sticks..........	8	20	Trace	Trace	4	1	.0	0	Trace	Trace	Trace	0
	Rice, cooked; 1 cup:												
351	Converted..........	72	205	4	Trace	45	14	.5	0	.10	.02	1.9	0
352	White..........	71	200	4	Trace	44	13	.5	0	.02	.01	.7	0
353	Rice, puffed, added thiamine, niacin, and iron; 1 ounce..........	5	110	2	Trace	25	4	.5	0	.12	.01	1.5	0
354	Rice flakes, added thiamine and niacin; 1 ounce..........	5	110	2	Trace	25	8	.6	0	.10	.01	1.6	0
	Rolls:												
	Plain, pan (16 ounces per dozen); 1 roll:												
355	Enriched..........	31	115	3	2	20	28	.7	Trace	.11	.07	.8	Trace
356	Unenriched..........	31	115	3	2	20	28	.3	Trace	.02	.03	.3	Trace
357	Hard, round (22 ounces per dozen); 1 roll..........	25	160	5	2	31	24	.4	Trace	.03	.05	.4	Trace
358	Sweet, pan (18 ounces per dozen); 1 roll..........	31	135	4	4	21	37	.3	30	.03	.06	.4	0
359	Spaghetti, cooked until tender; Enriched; 1 cup..........	72	155	5	1	32	11	1.3	0	.19	.11	1.5	0

9 Based on recipe using white cornmeal; if yellow cornmeal is used vitamin A value is 120 I.U.

10 Vitamin A based on yellow corn grits; white corn grits contain only a trace.

Item number	Food	Water	Food energy	Protein	Fat	Total carbohydrate	Calcium	Iron	Vitamin A value	Thiamine	Riboflavin	Niacin	Ascorbic acid
360	Unenriched; 1 cup	72	155	5	1	32	11	.6	0	.02	.02	.4	0
	Waffles, baked, with enriched flour:												
361	1 waffle (4½ by 5½ by ½ inches)	40	215	7	8	28	144	1.4	270	.14	.20	1.0	0
	Wheat, puffed:												
362	Added thiamine, niacin, and iron; 1 ounce	4	100	4	Trace	22	8	1.2	0	.16	.06	2.2	0
363	Presweetened, added thiamine and niacin; 1 ounce	3	105	1	Trace	26	4	.5	0	.12	.01	1.4	0
364	Wheat, rolled, cooked; 1 cup	80	175	5	1	40	19	1.7	0	.17	.06	2.1	0
365	Wheat, shredded, plain (long, round, or bite-size); 1 ounce	6	100	3	1	23	13	1.0	0	.06	.03	1.3	0
366	Wheat and malted barley cereal, added thiamine, niacin, and iron; 1 ounce	3	105	3	Trace	24	13	1.0	0	.13	.05	1.5	0
367	Wheat flakes, added thiamine, niacin, and iron; 1 ounce	4	100	3	Trace	23	13	1.2	0	.16	.05	1.8	0
	Wheat flours:												
368	Whole wheat; 1 cup, stirred	12	400	16	2	85	49	4.0	0	.66	.14	5.2	0
	All purpose or family flour:												
369	Enriched; 1 cup, sifted	12	400	12	1	84	18	[11]3.2	0	[11].48	[11].29	[11]3.8	0
370	Unenriched; 1 cup, sifted	12	400	12	1	84	18	.9	0	.07	.05	1.0	0
371	Wheat germ; 1 cup, stirred	11	245	17	7	34	57	5.5	0	1.39	.54	3.1	0
	FATS, OILS, RELATED PRODUCTS												
372	Butter; 1 tablespoon	16	100	Trace	11	Trace	3	0	[12]2,460				0
	Fats, cooking:												
	Vegetable fats:												
373	1 cup	0	1,770	0	200	0	0	0	0	0	0	0	0
374	1 tablespoon	0	110	0	12	0	0	0	0	0	0	0	0
	Lard:												
375	1 cup	0	1,985	0	220	0	0	0	0	0	0	0	0
376	1 tablespoon	0	125	0	14	0	0	0	0	0	0	0	0

SUGARS, SWEETS

No.	Food	Water (%)	Food energy (Cal.)	Protein (g)	Fat (g)	Carbohydrate (g)	Calcium (mg)	Iron (mg)	Vitamin A (I.U.)	Thiamine (mg)	Riboflavin (mg)	Niacin (mg)	Ascorbic acid (mg)
377	Margarine; 1 tablespoon	16	100	Trace	11	Trace	3	0	[13]460	...	...	...	0
378	Oils, salad or cooking; 1 tablespoon	0	125	0	14	0	0	0	0	0	0	0	0
	Salad dressings; 1 tablespoon:												
379	Blue cheese	28	90	1	10	1	11	Trace	30	Trace	.01	Trace	Trace
380	Commercial, plain (mayonnaise type)	48	60	Trace	6	2	Trace	Trace	30	Trace	Trace	Trace	Trace
381	French	42	60	Trace	6	2	Trace	Trace	0	Trace	0	Trace	0
382	Mayonnaise	14	110	Trace	12	Trace	3	.1	40	Trace	Trace	Trace	Trace
383	Thousand Island	38	75	1	8	1	2	.1	60	Trace	Trace	Trace	2
	Candy; 1 ounce:												
384	Caramels	7	120	1	3	22	36	.7	0	.01	.04	Trace	Trace
385	Chocolate, sweetened, milk	1	145	2	3	16	61	.3	50	.03	.11	.2	Trace
386	Fudge, plain	5	115	Trace	0	23	14	.3	Trace	Trace	.02	Trace	Trace
387	Hard	1	90	0	0	28	0	0	0	0	0	0	0
388	Marshmallow	15	40	Trace	Trace	11	3	0	0	0	0	0	0
389	Chocolate sirup; 1 tablespoon	39	60	Trace	Trace	17	...	.3	...	.01	Trace	.2	...
390	Honey, strained or extracted; 1 tablespoon	20	60	Trace	0	17	1	.2	0	Trace	.01	.1	1
391	Jams, marmalades, preserves; 1 tablespoon	28	55	Trace	Trace	14	2	.1	Trace	Trace	Trace	Trace	1
392	Jellies; 1 tablespoon	34	50	0	0	13	2	.1	Trace	Trace	Trace	Trace	1
	Molasses, cane; 1 tablespoon:												
393	Light	24	50	0	0	13	33	.9	0	.01	.01	Trace	...
394	Blackstrap	24	45	0	0	11	116	2.3	0	.02	.04	.3	...
395	Sirup, table blends; 1 tablespoon	25	55	0	0	15	9	.8	0	0	Trace	Trace	0
	Sugar; 1 tablespoon:												
396	Granulated, cane or beet	Trace	50	0	0	12	0	Trace	0	0	0	0	0
397	Brown	3	50	0	0	13	[14]10	.4	0	0	0	0	0

[11] Iron, thiamine, riboflavin, and niacin are based on the minimal level of enrichment specified in the standards of identity promulgated under the Federal Food, Drug, and Cosmetic Act.

[12] Year-round average.

[13] Based on the average vitamin A content of fortified margarine. Federal specifications for fortified margarine require a minimum of 15,000 I.U. of vitamin A per pound.

MISCELLANEOUS

Item number	Food	Water	Food energy	Protein	Fat	Total carbohydrate	Calcium	Iron	Vitamin A value	Thiamine	Riboflavin	Niacin	Ascorbic acid
398	Beverages, carbonated, kola type; 1 cup	88	105	...	...	28	...	...	...	...	...	...	...
399	Bouillon cubes; 1 cube	5	2	Trace	Trace	0	...	...	...	...	...	1.0	0
400	Chili sauce (mainly tomatoes); 1 tablespoon	69	15	Trace	Trace	4	2	.1	320	.02	.01	.4	2
401	Chocolate, unsweetened; 1 ounce	2	145	2	15	8	28	1.2	20	.01	.06	.3	0
402	Gelatin dessert, plain, ready-to-serve; 1 cup	83	155	4	0	36	0	...	0	...	0	0	0
	Olives, pickled: "Extra large" size, 12 olives or "Jumbo" size, 7 olives:												
403	Green	78	65	1	7	1	48	.9	170	Trace	Trace	...	...
404	Ripe	76	85	1	9	2	45	.9	40	Trace	Trace	...	...
	Pickles, cucumber:												
405	Dill; 1 large (4 inches long, 1¾-inch diameter)	93	15	1	Trace	3	34	1.6	420	Trace	.09	.1	8
406	Sweet; 1 pickle (2¾ inches long, ¾-inch diameter)	70	20	Trace	Trace	5	3	.3	20	0	Trace	Trace	1
407	Sherbet, factory packed; 1 cup (8-fluid-ounce container)	68	235	3	Trace	58	96	.1	0	.03	.15	.1	0
	Soups, ready-to-serve; 1 cup:												
408	Bean	82	190	8	5	30	95	2.8	...	.10	.10	.8	...
409	Beef	92	100	6	4	11	15	.5	...	...	...	...	...
410	Bouillon, broth, and consommé	95	10	2	...	0	20	1.0	0	0	.05	.6	0
411	Chicken	94	75	4	2	10	20	.5	...	0	.12	1.5	...
412	Clam chowder	91	85	5	2	12	36	3.6	...	.02	...	...	0
413	Cream soup (asparagus, celery, or mushroom)	85	200	7	12	18	217	.5	200	.05	.20	.1	0
414	Noodle, rice, or barley	90	115	6	4	13	82	.2	30	.02	.05	.7	0
415	Tomato	91	90	2	2	18	24	1.0	1,230	.02	.10	.7	10
416	Vegetable	92	80	4	2	14	32	.8	...	.05	.08	1.0	8
417	Vinegar; 1 tablespoon	...	2	0	...	1	1	...	...	...	...	...	...
418	White sauce, medium; 1 cup	73	430	10	33	23	305	.3	1,350	.07	.42	.3	1

14 Calcium value is based on dark brown sugar; value would be lower for light brown sugar.

Index

INDEX

Q

R

INDEX

*The best books on health and
nutrition are from*

LARCHMONT BOOKS

__"New High-Fiber Approach to Relieving Constipation
Naturally," by Adams and Murray; foreword by Sanford
O. Siegal, D.O., M.D.; 320 pages, $1.95

__"Program Your Heart for Health," by Frank Murray;
foreword by Michael Walczak, M.D., introduction by E.
Cheraskin, M.D., D.M.D.; 368 pages, $2.95.

__"Food for Beauty," by Helena Rubinstein; revised and
updated by Frank Murray, 256 pages, $1.95.

__"Eating in Eden," by Ruth Adams, 224 pages, $1.75.

__"Beverages," by Adams and Murray, 288 pages, $1.75.

__"Fighting Depression," by Harvey M. Ross, M.D.; 224
pages, $1.95.

__"Health Foods," by Ruth Adams and Frank Murray,
foreword by S. Marshall Fram, M.D.; 352 pages, $2.25.

__"Minerals: Kill or Cure?" by Ruth Adams and Frank
Murray; foreword by Harvey M. Ross, M.D.; 368 pages,
$1.95.

__"The Compleat Herbal," by Ben Charles Harris, 252
pages, $1.75.